A COMPANION GUIDE TO LIFE SENTENCES

2ND EDITION

NIGEL STONE

REVISED BY NEIL STONE

Shaw & Sons

A Companion Guide to Life Sentences
Second Edition

Published by
Shaw & Sons Limited
Shaway House
21 Bourne Park
Bourne Road
Crayford
Kent DA1 4BZ

www.shaws.co.uk

© Shaw & Sons Limited 2008

Published March 2008
(First edition published 1997 by Owen Wells Publisher)

ISBN 978 0 7219 1622 4

A CIP catalogue record for this book is
available from the British Library

Printed in Great Britain by
Antony Rowe Limited, Chippenham

SUMMARY OF CONTENTS

TABLE OF CONTENTS

FOREWORD

There has been significant change in the criminal justice arena during the decade since the first edition of this book was published. Six Home Secretaries have presided over three influential reports – those of Auld, Halliday and Carter. The new Criminal Justice Act and the Offender Management Act 2007 have been introduced. This past decade has also seen the creation of the National Offender Management Service (NOMS), the introduction of Offender Management and the amalgamation of Magistrates' and Crown Court Services into Her Majesty's Court Service (HMCS). In May 2007 the Probation Service left the Home Office and joined the newly formed Ministry of Justice firstly under Lord Faulkner and latterly Jack Straw MP. Furthermore, the prison population has continued to rise inexorably to unprecedented levels with the lifer population increasing almost threefold from 3,517 to 9,351.

In the foreword to the first edition, Nigel Stone described how the management and supervision of lifers presents criminal justice professionals with major anxieties in risk assessment. The stress of dealing with those who have committed the most heinous, repulsive and most worrying of crimes continues to be a major challenge. An updated *Companion Guide to Life Sentences* which addresses some of the complexities of working with life-sentenced prisoners is much needed.

Much has been made of the shift in the value base of the Probation Service away from its roots in court missionaries who 'used inquiry, friendship and personal influence to govern offenders' (Vanstone, 2004). Many within the Probation Service, myself included, believe that we should be proud of our history of concerning ourselves with 'moral good' driven by humanitarian values (Celnick & McWilliams, 1991). It is to these probation colleagues – who carry out one of the most difficult and least understood tasks of all the criminal justice agencies – that I dedicate this book. Additional thanks to Liz and Charlotte and colleagues in South Wales Probation Area and HM Prison Service who gave their advice and expertise freely. The errors and omissions though, regretfully, remain mine.

Neil Stone

GLOSSARY

AC	Appeal Cases (House of Lords)
ACO	Assistant Chief Officer
Admin LR	Administrative Law Reports
AG	Advice to Governors
All ER	All England Reports
AUCG	Allocations Unit, Control Group
BA	Bail Act 1976
BMLR	Butterworths Medico-Legal Reports
CAA	Criminal Appeals Act 1968, 1995
CCRC	Criminal Cases Review Commission
CI	Circular Instruction
CJ	Lord Chief Justice
CJA	Criminal Justice Act 1982, 1991, 2003
CJPOA	Criminal Justice and Public Order Act 1994
CPO	Chief Probation Officer
CYPA	Children and Young Persons Act 1933, 1969
Crim LR	Criminal Law Review
Cr App R	Criminal Appeal Reports
Cr App R(S)	Criminal Appeal Reports (Sentencing)
DLP	Discretionary Lifer Panel
DLU	Discretionary Lifer Unit
EHRR	European Human Rights Reports
HA	Homicide Act 1957
HMP	HM Prison, Detention at Her Majesty's Pleasure
HOC	Home Office Circular
I	Instruction to Governors
IPP	Imprisonment for Public Protection
J	High Court Judge
LJ	Lord Justice of Appeal
LLO	Lifer Liaison Officer
LM	Lifer Manual
LSP	Life Sentence Plan
LSRB	Life Sentence Review Board
M(ADP)A	Murder (Abolition of the Death Penalty) Act 1965

MHA	Mental Health Act 1983
MHRT	Mental Health Review Tribunal
MLU	Mandatory Lifer Unit
MR	Master of the Rolls
NIB	National Identification Bureau, Scotland Yard
NOMS	National Offender Management Service
NPS	National Probation Service
OASys	Offender Assessment System
OM	Offender Manager
PAS	Prisoners' Advice Service
PBR	Parole Board Rules 1992
PC	Probation Circular
PLRG	Parole and Lifer Review Group
PPG	Penile Plethysmograph
PRD	Provisional Release Date
PRES	Pre-Release Employment Scheme
PSOS	Prison Service Operating Standards
QB	Queen's Bench Division
ROA	Rehabilitation of Offenders Act 1974
RSC	Rules of the Supreme Court
SOTP	Sex Offender Treatment Programme
WLR	Weekly Law Reports

1
INTRODUCTION

In his book *Responses to Crime*, Lord Windlesham, former Home Office Minister and Chair of the Parole Board 1982–88, devoted a chapter to 'Life Imprisonment: A Sentence Nobody Can Understand?'. In further accounts (1989 and 1993), the same author traced what he describes as 'a very sorry chapter in the history of English criminal law and its administration' since the abolition of the death penalty in 1965. He describes 'the paradox now posed by life imprisonment – neither a sentence for life nor a genuinely indeterminate term'. This confusion will be shared by practitioners and by the lifers they work with, particularly as the ground rules of life sentences appear in constant flux. Many lifers will have experienced episodes of this 'sorry chapter' in the course of their sentence careers. It may therefore be helpful to try to summarise the recent history to provide a better understanding of the key themes of the story: the oscillating divide between mandatory and discretionary life sentences; the tension between executive and judicial decision-making in interpreting the meaning of 'life', a tension which Shute (2006) refers to as 'an increasingly acrimonious tussle'; the growth in a 'bureaucratic-lawful' approach (Barak-Glanty, 1981) (*ie* greater fairness, openness and consistency) to managing lifers; an increasing emphasis on more systematic risk assessment in life sentence planning.

The media furore surrounding the sentencing of Craig Sweeney (*R v Sweeney*, 2006) best exemplifies the fact that the confusion referred to by Lord Windlesham fourteen years ago still exists. Sweeney was sentenced to life imprisonment for offences of kidnap and assault of a child under 13 by penetration on three occasions. When sentencing Sweeney, Judge Griffith Williams took into account the need to determine the minimum term to be served for punishment (s82A of the Powers of Criminal Courts (Sentencing) Act 2000), which is how long an offender receiving a determinate sentence for the same offence would serve in prison. The starting point is half of the length of the notional determinate sentence since a determinate sentence prisoner serves half of their sentence in the community. Sweeney pleaded guilty and this was taken into account, as was the time he had already spent on remand. Judge Williams concluded that the seriousness of the offence would warrant an 18-year determinate sentence which he then reduced by one-third to 12 years to take into account the guilty plea. He then halved the remainder and, after deduction of time served on remand, this left a period of 5 years and 108 days.

In his remarks Judge Williams said: 'It will only be after you have served that period (5 years, 108 days) that the Parole Board will be entitled to consider your release. It will only be when it is satisfied that you need no longer be

1

imprisoned for the protection of the public that it will be able to direct your release'. He went on to say that 'the public should understand that an early release in your case is unlikely'. It was these last words that went largely unreported and the figure of 5 years and 108 days that dominated the headlines. The *Daily Telegraph* of 13 June 2006 was typical of the coverage in its headline, 'Outcry as abductor of girl, 3, is given 5 years'. Within hours of passing the sentence, the Crown Prosecution Service asked Lord Goldsmith (the Attorney General) to raise the case with the Court of Appeal and the Home Secretary, John Reid, weighed in to the debate by sending a letter of concern to the Attorney General.

The Government was so anxious about the impact of public perception regarding life sentences that they ordered a review of the way offenders are sentenced to indeterminate sentences (*Making Sentences Clearer*, 2006) and asked the Sentencing Guidelines Council to consider whether judges should be able to reduce or remove the discount for an early guilty plea when the evidence against the defendant is overwhelming. In January 2007, the Sentencing Guidelines Council concluded that discounts should still be given: however, offenders who face 'an overwhelming prosecution case' should see the maximum of their term trimmed from one-third to one-fifth.

A SHORT HISTORY OF LIFE SENTENCE REVIEW
Standard Practice up to 1972
Until 1972, the general practice was to refer all cases to the Parole Board not later than seven years after sentence.

Initial Assessment by Committee
For the next decade until 1983, a more discriminating procedure was adopted. A Joint Committee of senior Parole Board members and Home Office officials made an initial assessment of all life sentences after three or four years of sentence and either set a date for the lifer's first review or, in cases where this was not yet considered appropriate, fixed a date for a further consideration by the Joint Committee.

The Secretary of State and the Tariff
In 1983, Leon Brittan as Home Secretary disbanded the Joint Committee and announced that the Home Secretary would in future determine the date for the lifer's first review, after consulting the trial judge and Lord Chief Justice (some three years after sentence) 'on the requirements of retribution and deterrence' in the individual case, first review normally taking place three years before the expiry of the period deemed necessary to meet those requirements. In addition, certain types of mandatory lifer would not normally be released until a minimum 20 years had been served.

This was a significant development, because it made explicit for the first time that the life sentence consisted of an initial period necessary to satisfy demands of retribution and deterrence (the 'tariff' term), followed by such further period reflecting an unacceptable risk posed to the public. The judiciary were assigned a role limited to the former issue and the Parole Board were to concentrate on risk, while the ultimate discretion both as regards the determination of tariff and the judgment of acceptable risk rested with the Home Secretary.

The Handscomb Judgment

In the pioneering decision of *R v Secretary of State for the Home Department, ex parte Handscomb* (1988) 86 Cr App R 59, the Divisional Court held that, for discretionary lifers, consultation with the judiciary should take place as soon as practicable after sentence and that the Home Secretary should abide by the views of the judiciary regarding retribution and deterrence, *ie* a period equivalent to the notional determinate sentence for the crime in question, less one third remission to which the determinate prisoner would then be entitled. In a subsequent Parliamentary statement, the Home Secretary (Douglas Hurd) indicated that Handscomb would be put into effect by asking the trial judge to write to him via the Lord Chief Justice. First review would begin three years before the time when the lifer would have served two-thirds of the notional determinate sentence. Thus if the judicial tariff was 12 years, review would begin after five years. The Home Secretary agreed to accept the judicial view on tariff and not revise this by interposing his own judgment (though this part of the Handscomb judgment was later overruled by the Court of Appeal in 1992).

This milestone decision thus established a clear distinction between mandatory and discretionary lifers. The Home Secretary decided that mandatory lifers would follow suit in the sense that the views of the trial judge and Lord Chief Justice could in future be obtained as soon as possible after sentence but, because there was no question of a notional determinate sentence for the crime of murder, the Minister reserved the right to set the tariff term, taking into account other factors such as the public acceptability of release and the need to maintain public confidence in the criminal justice system.

Challenging Executive Discretion

In the following year, in *R v Home Secretary, ex parte Benson* (1988), *The Times*, 21 November, the Divisional Court considered the test which the Parole Board and the Home Secretary should apply in determining the degree of risk to the public when reviewing a tariff-expired discretionary lifer. This was the first occasion that a lifer had successfully challenged the Home Secretary's exercise of discretion in refusing to accept a recommendation for release from the Parole Board.

House of Lords Report, 1989

The House of Lords Select Committee on Murder and Life Imprisonment published a report in 1989 arguing that the sentence for murder should no longer be fixed but should be at the discretion of the court, which would pass whichever sentence was appropriate for the circumstances of the offence and the offender, whether life imprisonment, a determinate prison sentence or a hospital order. The Committee was not impressed by the argument that murder is a 'uniquely serious offence'. The Committee also proposed that where a life sentence was imposed, the judge would have to specify reasons for not imposing a determinate sentence and would specify in open court the period of years considered necessary to satisfy requirements of retribution and deterrence. This would not be subject to revision by the Home Secretary but would be appealable. Release decisions on expiry of the penal term would be made by a judicial tribunal composed of a High Court judge, a consultant psychiatrist and a Chief Probation Officer. This Report subsequently inspired a series of unsuccessful amendments to the Criminal Justice Bill which became the Criminal Justice Act 1991.

The Thynne Judgment

Following protracted consideration from 1985, the European Court of Human Rights in *Thynne and Others v UK* upheld the claim of three discretionary lifers that their continued lawful detention following tariff expiry should have been determined by a judicial authority, further to Article 5.4 of the European Convention (see page 12).

Discretionary Lifer Panels

In response to the *Thynne* ruling, the Criminal Justice Act 1991 amended the procedures relating to discretionary life sentences, introducing both the trial judge's responsibility to determine the penal term for the offence and also the Discretionary Lifer Panel procedure for assessing risk in a quasi-judicial manner. It was thus confirmed that issues of 'public acceptability' are not relevant in determining the release of discretionary lifers. The Government refused to change the basis for dealing with mandatory life sentences, arguing that murder is such a grave offence that the offender forfeits their liberty for life without the necessity for judicial intervention. 'The presumption is therefore that the offender should remain in custody unless and until the Home Secretary concludes that the public interest would be better served by the prisoner's release than by their continued detention' (Home Office Minister Angela Rumbold, House of Commons, 16 July 1991).

The Doody Judgment

In June 1993, The House of Lords in *ex parte Doody* gave mandatory lifers the right to know the minimum period which the trial judge thought that they should serve and the gist of the reasons why that recommendation was made, together with the right to make representations before the tariff is set and to be informed of the reasons for any departure from the judge's recommendation when the tariff is set. The Lords affirmed that the Home Secretary was not obliged to adopt the judicial view because Parliament had entrusted the task of deciding a mandatory lifer's release to the Executive. Any change in these provisions would be a matter for the Legislative.

The Howard Approach

In July 1993 the then Home Secretary, Michael Howard, reiterated Angela Rumbold's account of the mandatory life sentence, dismissing arguments suggesting that discretionary and mandatory lifers should be dealt with on a similar basis. He also asserted that the Home Secretary can revise tariff terms for mandatory lifers upwards if the term earlier fixed is subsequently deemed insufficient to satisfy requirements of deterrence and retribution and that mandatory lifers who have served their tariff period and are not considered to present a danger to the public if released may nevertheless continue to be detained if release would not be 'acceptable to the public'.

The Wynne Judgment

In *Wynne v United Kingdom* (1994) the European Court accepted the UK's argument that 'the mandatory life sentence belongs to a different category from the discretionary sentence' and that, 'while the two types of life sentence may be converging, there remains a substantial gap between them'. Consequently, the release of a mandatory lifer is entirely a matter for the Home Secretary who is not bound by the judicial recommendations as to the length of the tariff and who can have regard to criteria other than dangerousness, following the expiry of the tariff period, in deciding on release.

Home Affairs Committee on Murder

In December 1995, the House of Commons Select Committee on Home Affairs Report *Murder: The Mandatory Life Sentence* concluded that life imprisonment should remain the mandatory sentence for murder but reached the 'preliminary conclusion' that responsibility for setting the tariff and taking decisions on release should be removed from the Home Secretary. The Committee invited further evidence as to how a workable system might be constructed to put these two conclusions into compatible effect. In its supplementary report of June 1996, the Committee confirmed its preliminary conclusions, proposing that the trial judge's tariff proposal should be announced in open court at time of sentence, allowing the defence and the Attorney General the opportunity to appeal against that recommendation. The Court of Appeal would thus have the final authority to determine the tariff term. Lifer panels of the Parole Board would subsequently have the power to direct the release of mandatory lifers.

In a response to the Committee (published 5 August 1996), the Government has rejected this recommendation, arguing that such a move would reduce public confidence in the criminal justice system, prevent direct accountability to Parliament for decisions on tariff and release, and limit the proper breadth of consideration in such decisions.

HMPs

In February 1996, the European Court ruled that persons sentenced for murder and ordered to be detained during Her Majesty's pleasure because of their age at the time of the offence should not be treated on the same basis as other mandatory lifers but are entitled to have the lawfulness of their detention judicially reviewed in the same way as discretionary lifers (*Hussain v United Kingdom*). The European Court ruled that under Article 5(4) of the Convention, prisoners detained at Her Majesty's pleasure were entitled to have the lawfulness of their continued detention determined by a judicial or quasi-judicial body. The UK Government, in response to this ruling, introduced s28 of the (Crime Sentences) Act 1997, which placed the release decision into the remit of Discretionary Lifer Panels. This section, however, did not change the release procedures for adult murderers.

Thompson and Venables (2000)

When Jon Venables and Robert Thompson were convicted of the murder of James Bulger in 1993, they received an indeterminate sentence of detention under Her Majesty's pleasure. The minimum period was set by the Home Secretary. Challenged at the European Court of Human Rights, the Court decided that the role of the Home Secretary in fixing tariffs for juvenile murderers sentenced to Her Majesty's pleasure was in breach of Article 6(1) of the Convention. Following this ruling, the Government were obliged to bring in legislation transferring the Home Secretary's tariff setting role for murderers under the age of 18 to the sentencing judge in open court (s60 Criminal Justice and Court Services Act 2000).

The Stafford Ruling

In *Stafford v UK 2002*, the European Court of Human Rights ruled that the parole board had to have the power to order release where it determined release was appropriate. The Court consequently ruled therefore that the Home Secretary's veto of a Parole Board's recommendation that a post-tariff lifer should be released contravened Articles 5(1) and 5(4) of the European Convention.

R v Anderson 2003

When this case was considered by the House of Lords they ruled that the power of the Home Secretary to set minimum terms in murder cases where the defendant was aged 18 or over was incompatible with Article 6 of the Human Rights Convention. The Government responded by introducing measures in the

Criminal Justice Act 2003 to transfer the power to fix tariffs in mandatory lifer cases from the Home Secretary to sentencing judges whilst issuing statutory guidelines which have to be taken into account when the Judge sets a minimum term. These guidelines can be found in ss 269-277 of, and Sch 21 to, the Act. Shute (2006) describes these guidelines, which came into effect in December 2003, as controversial, in that political control over the meaning of mandatory life sentences is re-established and cites the announcement of the then Home Secretary, David Blunkett, 'Parliament retained the paramount role in setting a clear framework for dealing with the most dangerous and evil people in our society'. In this extract from his diaries, David Blunkett reveals the determination of both the judiciary and politicians to gain control of life sentencing at the time of the passage of the Criminal Justice Bill through the House of Lords:

> 'I'd had a definitive meeting in the room off my office where I decided what the (sentencing) terms should be that we lay down in the Criminal Justice and Sentencing Bill. They then come back, having been gone over by the Lord Chancellor's Department and the judiciary, recommending far lower sentences to the fixed terms that I had already determined we should stick to ... They were proposing three tariffs: life (because I'd indicated life meant life so there was nothing they could do about that) for absolutely horrendous crimes; twenty years for things like killing a policeman or even a second murder that wasn't judged to be horrendous; and twelve years for other murders, which I've now upped to thirty years and twenty years respectively. This was based on the fact that previous tariffs given by home secretaries had been in the lower range and that judges would try to lower the figure, whereas if we set a low figure as the commencement, they would raise the figure. You have to be beyond naivety to believe that what you need to do is set a low figure so that the judges will increase it. I have overturned that, but it just goes to show what goes on.'

> (Blunkett, 2006)

The Lord Chief Justice, Lord Phillips, has expressed his unease at the effect these tariff guidelines will have on both the sentenced prisoners and the prison population. He told an audience of academics in Birmingham that, as a result of the changes brought about by the CJA 2003, prisons would be 'full of geriatric lifers'. Lord Phillips went on to say:

> 'If sentencing is to be just, then the effect of mitigating and aggravating factors should be very significant, so the sentences fill the spectrum between these two starting points. I am not sure in practice they do, and I believe that the starting points are having the effect of racketing up sentences in a manner that will be regretted in many years to come'

> (*The Telegraph*, 10 March 2007)

There are two significant factors left to consider in this broad vista sweep of the life sentences. One is the overwhelming weight of professional opinion in the criminal justice system which favours the abolition of the mandatory life sentence; whether that may be the Advisory Council on the Penal System in 1978, former Lord Chief Justice Lord Lane (1993), the Penal Affairs Consortium (1994), the Prison Governors Association (1995), Justice in 1996 and, more recently, the Law Commission in its report, *Partial Defences to Murder* (2004). Politicians of all political parties show no desire to abolish the mandatory sentence and this seems even less so as we enter another period of a 'risk averse' criminal justice system. The final factor is not related to the legal framework but to the creative management of the lifer system. The assessment and reduction of risk, always at the least a notional feature of lifer careers and review, has grown in prominence and sophistication, both to enhance public confidence and increase public protection. Sentence planning and reviews, judgments about suitability for transfer, temporary release, release on licence and recall have all acquired greater detail, care and alertness. The advent of Discretionary Lifer Panels (DLPs) has served to quicken this momentum. The inclusion of Imprisonment for Public Protection (IPP) lifers into mainstream Offender Management in January 2008 – known as phase 3 – will entail a greater emphasis on a single point of contact in the home probation service, an Offender Manager, who will be responsible for risk assessment and management of the lifer using the Offender Assessment System (OASys), chairing sentence planning meetings and having a greater input than previously into the lifer's sentence.

The remainder of this Introduction sketches the primary routes which enable life sentence administration to receive independent judicial scrutiny.

JUDICIAL REVIEW

The opportunity to seek judicial review of administrative decisions (through the Administrative Court (which is part of the High Court)), made in respect of prisoners' lives, has become of major importance in recent years as the judiciary have shown increasing willingness to intervene in the regulation of imprisonment, allowing independent scrutiny of all aspects of prison life from categorisation, segregation, adjudication and transfers to the calculation of sentence length and access to medical treatment. There are four grounds which can give rise to applications under judicial review: illegality, irrationality, procedural impropriety and incompatibility with European Convention. Lifers have gained particularly from this opportunity because of the executive discretion exercised in crucial aspects of their liberty (actual and potential). As Creighton and King (1996) observe:

> 'In particular, the mandatory life sentence system has been the subject of repeated attack and the court has taken it upon itself to provide strict

regulation of a sentence which has attracted strong criticism from all levels of the judiciary.'

Comments by Steyn LJ in *R v Secretary of State for the Home Department, ex parte Pegg* (1994) *The Times*, 11 August are particularly indicative of this attitude:

'Given the essential unfairness of the system in relation to prisoners serving mandatory life sentences, the courts have to bear in mind that fundamental rights are at stake. But courts can do no more than to be extra vigilant in the exercise of their powers of judicial review.'

Procedure

Applications for judicial review are initiated by an application for leave to apply, which is considered by a single High Court judge, either on the basis of the papers or at an oral hearing. If the application for leave proceeds with an oral hearing, the respondent (*eg* the Secretary of State or the Parole Board) may well seek to appear or may be invited to attend. The judge has to be satisfied that there is an arguable case for review, that the applicant has sufficient interest in the outcome and that there has not been any undue delay in making application. Applications should be made 'promptly' and, in any event, within three months of the date when the grounds for application arose (RSC Order 53 r4). If a 'paper' application is unsuccessful, the applicant may renew their application to a judge in open court (unless the court directs that the application should be renewed to a Divisional Court (consisting of two judges)). If leave has been refused after an oral hearing, the application may be renewed to the Court of Appeal. If the Court of Appeal refuses leave, the application fails.

If leave is granted, the substantive application will come before a single judge unless the case is directed to be heard by a Divisional Court. If the Court of Appeal granted leave on a renewed leave application, that Court can reserve the application to itself.

Following the substantive hearing and decision before a single judge or a Divisional Court, either an unsuccessful applicant or a respondent whose decision has been successfully challenged may appeal to the Court of Appeal. A further appeal may be made to the House of Lords in exceptional cases on a point of general public importance (*eg* as in *ex parte Doody*), provided that either the Court of Appeal or the House of Lords grants leave for this final stage to proceed. Though there is normally no intermediate right of appeal to the Court of Appeal in a criminal case (Supreme Court Act 1981 s18(1)), applications by lifers in respect of the Home Secretary's or Parole Board's exercise of discretion are classified as civil for judicial review purposes.

Legal Aid is available for judicial review proceedings. *Judicial Review Proceedings* by Jonathan Manning (1995) provides a detailed guide to the relevant procedure.

Principles

Many examples of judicial review, sought in respect of decisions by both the Home Secretary and the Parole Board, are given in Chapters 7, 8 and 9. In particular, in *R v Secretary of State for the Home Department, ex parte Doody* [1994] 1 AC 531, Lord Mustill in the House of Lords identified six general principles promoting openness and fairness:

(i)   Where an Act of Parliament confers an administrative power, there is a presumption that it will be exercised in a manner which is fair in all the circumstances.

(ii) The standards of fairness are not immutable. They may change with the passage of time, both in the general and in their application to decisions of a particular type.

(iii) The principles of fairness are not to be applied by rote identically in every situation. What fairness demands is dependent on the context of the decision.

(iv) An essential feature of the context is the statute which creates the discretion, as regards both its language and the shape of the legal and administrative system within which the decision is taken.

(v) Fairness will very often require that a person who may be adversely affected by the decision will have an opportunity to make representations on their own behalf, either before the decision is taken with a view to producing a favourable result, or after it is taken, with a view to procuring its modification, or both.

(vi) Since the person affected usually cannot make worthwhile representations without knowing what factors may weigh against their interests, fairness will very often require that s/he is informed of the gist of the case which s/he has to answer.

Decisions not only have to be fair, within the decision-maker's powers and in accord with principles of natural justice, but also 'reasonable', though the courts have indicated that they will only interfere with the substance of the decision if it is one 'no reasonable body could have come to', a test usually referred to as '*Wednesbury* unreasonable' (after the case of *Associated Picture Houses Ltd v Wednesbury Corporation* [1948] 1 KB 223 which set out this criterion).

The remedy of judicial review does not provide an appeal against an unfavourable administrative or regulatory decision and does not allow the court to substitute its own decision for that which is being challenged. It simply allows the court to identify unlawful, unfair or unreasonable decisions and, where appropriate, to require the decision-making body to make a fresh determination in accordance with the law. The following considerations seek to summarise the other bounds of the remedy:

- Judicial review is a discretionary remedy and, even if a case is eligible for relief, the court is not obliged to grant it. 'It is important to consider the purpose of the application and whether, even if there is no practical remedy available, there is a point of law that is important enough to warrant the intervention of the court' (Creighton and King, 1996).

- The court will not normally consider an application if there is another avenue allowing the adverse decision to be reconsidered. Judicial review is thus a 'last resort' remedy, but for lifers faced with an adverse decision by the Home Secretary or the Parole Board, judicial review will be appropriate because there is no formal right of appeal against that decision.

- Prisoners are not required to complain to the Prison Ombudsman before applying for judicial review because the Ombudsman has only an advisory capacity. Note also that the Prison Ombudsman has no power to investigate Parole Board decisions as these are not decisions of the Prison Service, nor ministerial decisions about the review and release of lifers (see also page 45).

EUROPEAN CONVENTION ON HUMAN RIGHTS

The European Convention on Human Rights was incorporated into all forms of UK law through the Human Rights Act of 1998.

Applications made under the Convention have had a considerable impact on the prison system and the rights of prisoners. We have seen earlier in this chapter the impact of challenges under Article 6 (applicable to the setting of the tariff); of equal significance have been Articles 5(1) and (4):

(1) Everyone has the right to liberty and security of person. No-one shall be deprived of his liberty save in the following cases and in accordance with a procedure prescribed by law:

    (a) the lawful detention of a person after conviction by a competent court

    ...

(4) Everyone who is deprived of his liberty by arrest or detention shall be entitled to take proceedings by which the lawfulness of his detention shall be decided speedily by a court and his release ordered if the detention is not lawful.

The first successful challenge of Parole Board review procedures for non-compliance with Article (5)4 was *Weeks v UK* (1987) 10 EHRR 293, decided on the somewhat unusual facts of a 17-year-old sentenced to life for an incompetent robbery. Released after 10 years but recalled a year later, Mr Weeks was released and recalled on numerous occasions over the next decade, spending a further six years in custody. In *Thynne, Wilson and Gunnell v UK* (1990) 13 EHRR 666, Article 5(4) was interpreted to afford all discretionary lifers the right to have their continued detention determined by a judicial hearing, causing the introduction of discretionary lifer panels, as detailed in Chapter 8. More recently (in *Hussain and Singh v UK*, 1996) the Court has determined that the domestic procedures for the review of persons detained at Her Majesty's pleasure violated Article 5(4) (see Chapter 7). On the other hand, the Court has upheld the distinction drawn between mandatory and discretionary lifers and confirmed that mandatory lifers have no right of review before a judicial body (*Wynne v UK*, 1994). The timescale for applications is inevitably somewhat protracted but this is less of a disincentive for long-term prisoners and lifers in particular.

Applications Procedure

Claims that rights guaranteed under the Convention have been violated can be examined by two bodies established under the Convention, the Commission for Human Rights and the European Court of Human Rights.

Applications are made initially to the Commission which decides whether an application is admissible, on the basis of three criteria:

(i) Has the application been made within the relevant time limits (*ie* within six months of the alleged violation or the exhaustion of domestic remedies)?

(ii) Have all domestic remedies been exhausted (though this does not mean that in all instances the applicant has to have sought judicial review if that would provide an effective remedy)?

(iii) Is the application manifestly ill-founded (*ie* does the application disclose a *prima facie* breach of the Convention)?

After an initial investigation by the Commission, an oral hearing may be held both on the issue of admissibility and the merits of the application. If the application is declared inadmissible, that concludes the initiative and there is no right of appeal. If an application is considered admissible, the Commission prepares a preliminary report on the merits and seeks proposals from the applicant and respondent Member State to try to achieve a settlement. If a settlement cannot be secured, the Commission publishes its detailed decision on the merits of the application. Either the Commission or the Member State concerned can refer the matter to the Court. The individual applicant cannot require reference of the case to the Court. Under the Commission's legal aid provision, financial help is available only from the time that an applicant is asked to make written submissions in reply to the Member State's observations, and aid is not available for the initial application.

If reference is made to the Court, the Court will normally inquire whether the parties want an oral hearing or for the application to be adjudicated on the basis of written representations. The Court normally accepts the findings of fact reached by the Commission but is not bound to do so. The Court reaches its decisions by majority. It has discretionary power to award compensation where it finds a violation but may well conclude that its decision alone is an adequate remedy.

2
PRE-SENTENCE PHASE

This chapter comprises a miscellany of provisions applicable to prospective life sentence cases prior to sentence, in respect of Probation Service responsibilities, provisions for bail and medical assessments, etc.

PROBATION SUPERVISEES CHARGED WITH SERIOUS FURTHER OFFENCES (SFO)

The revised notification and review procedures contained within Probation Circular 41/2006 introduce a rigorous system for scrutiny for cases where offenders under the supervision of the Probation Service have been charged with murder or a serious violent or sexual offence. This includes residence at Approved Premises. The purpose of the SFO procedure is to identify and disseminate areas of continuous improvement to risk assessment zand management and inform Ministers, the Chief Executive of NOMS and Regional Managers of cases of serious further offences. Responsibility for the operation of the SFO procedure lies with the Public Protection Unit SFO Team.

The following offenders are eligible:

- those who are under any form of supervision by the Probation Service;

- those whose supervision ended within 20 working days of the SFO;

- those for whom a warrant for breach of supervision has been issued within three months of the date of the SFO;

- those who are under supervision and charged with an equivalent eligible offence in another jurisdiction; and

- those who meet the criteria but have died prior to being charged.

Offence Eligibility

There are 47 eligible violent offences and 29 specified sexual offences. All are contained within Annexe A of the Probation Circular 41/2006. The case can only be recorded as an SFO when the offender and offence eligibility are met and the harm to the victim is serious, *ie* resulting in death/life-threatening and/or traumatic (from which recovery, be it physical or psychological, can be expected to be difficult or impossible). The case will also be an SFO where the offence and offender criteria are not met, but where the offence attracts significant national public interest – broadly defined in the SFO User Guide as when the case impacts upon national policy or the national reputation of NOMS or other part of the criminal justice system. A case does not become an SFO if an offender is subject to life licence but the supervision has been suspended at the time of the SFO. In this instance the Probation Area may decide to carry out an internal review in order to contribute to any review carried out by the Lifer Board.

Probation Areas are required to appoint a single point of administrative contact and nominate a lead senior operational manager to manage the co-ordination of SFO reviews. Notification of SFOs to the Public Protection Unit should occur within ten working days of the first Court appearance. There are seven review stages, with most cases being handled at Stage 3 (Initial Review) or Stage 4 (Full Review). Only in exceptional circumstances would a Stage 7 (Independent Review) be carried out and this would reflect concerns regarding poor management of cases or where the Full Review failed to address areas of improvement or poor staff performance.

Death or Serious Abuse of Children

When the SFO eligibility criteria are met, and a Serious Case Review (Working Together to Safeguard Children), formerly known as 'Part Eight Reviews', is to be undertaken by the Local Safeguarding Children Board (LSCB), a Stage 4 (Full Review) is required. The Probation Area must share a summary of the findings from the Full Review with the LSCB.

PROBATION SERVICE RESPONSIBILITIES

The life sentence prisoner can expect to have contact with the National Probation Service (NPS) throughout their period in prison from remand to release and whilst under supervision on life licence. As *LM* para. 1.10 indicates, the management of lifers will involve a number of agencies beyond the Prison and Probation Service and multi-agency working is essential when managing life sentence prisoners. Early identification of some potential lifers may be problematical, particularly in the case where the prospect of a sentence for IPP may be handed down: however, this is not certain until actual sentencing takes place. Many likely life sentence prisoners can, however, be identified.

Opening a File

In every instance of a possible life sentence, an Offender Manager (OM) must be appointed in the defendant's home area. In the case of itinerant defendants of 'no fixed abode', the 'home area' may need to be negotiated or, alternatively, the task should be undertaken within the probation team covering the area of the alleged offence and prosecution. Once appointed, the Offender Manager should open a file containing:

- press cuttings showing local reaction to the alleged offence;

- a record of preliminary contacts with the prisoner on remand;
- a record of contact with family or friends.

Should the defendant be acquitted, the file should be destroyed.

Role of Seconded Probation Staff

Chapter 4 of the Lifer Manual sets out what is expected of remand centres and local prisons in the management of potential, sentenced and recalled lifers. Life sentence prisoners (on remand and sentenced) will be placed before a reception board on their arrival into custody. Seconded probation officers must be members of the establishment's lifer management team (*LM* para. 4.3.6). The seconded prison probation officer participates in the board and will see the lifer later that day or the next day for an induction interview, during which it will be established as to whether the prisoner has any specific needs or whether there are people outside who may need support. The prison Lifer Officer will be the main contact for the prisoner in these early days. Special attention needs to be paid to the possibility of suicide at this time because of the nature of the offence and, if found guilty, its likely outcome. Where appropriate, contact should be made with the Offender Manager in the 'home' area, with the prison probation officer playing a pro-active role. A lifer plan (LISP1A) should be opened which includes all information relevant to the case and which logs all contact with the offender.

Pre-Sentence Reports in Murder Cases

In cases where a discretionary life sentence may be passed and a guilty plea is anticipated, a pre-sentence report will be prepared in the conventional way. The report should be in a Standard Delivery Report (SDR) format and generated by a Full OASys. In murder cases where the defendant will almost certainly be pleading not guilty, it is not appropriate to prepare a pre-trial report, irrespective of intended plea. If a defendant is convicted of murder, the only possible discretion available to the judge would be whether to recommend a minimum period for which the offender should be detained; the judge will almost certainly base any such recommendation on the evidence given and impressions gained during the trial. If the defendant is convicted of a lesser charge, primarily manslaughter either on grounds of diminished responsibility or some other basis for culpable homicide, it would be for the judge to indicate post-conviction whether a pre-sentence report is required.

Provision of a Pre-Sentence Report in the Sentencing of Dangerous Offenders

Provisions contained within the CJA 2003 regarding dangerous offenders came into force on April 2005. An offender is dangerous within the meaning of Chapter 5 of the Act if, following conviction of a specified offence, the court decides that there is a significant risk of serious harm from him/her by the commission of further specified offences. Specified offences are defined in s224(1) of, and listed in Sch 15 to, the CJA 2003. Section 156(3)(a) of the Act requires a court to obtain a pre-sentence report (PSR) before forming any opinion on risk which would, in turn, inform sentencing under the provisions, unless the court believes no question of significant risk arises or the offender is so obviously dangerous as for it to be indisputable.

If the court agrees that the offender is dangerous, it must impose one of three types of sentence:

(1) Life imprisonment (but only for offences that carry life).

(2) Imprisonment for public protection (IPP) (for offences carrying ten years or more).

(3) Extended sentence.

The NPS Guide on new sentences for public protection states:

'6.2.6   The PSR in all cases should address the type of information listed in s229(2) and 229(3) and meet the requirements of a Standard Delivery PSR as set out in Probation Circular 18/2005: Criminal Justice Act 2003 New Sentences and the New Report Framework.'

PSR authors may also find the following lengthy extract from *R v Lang* ([2005] EWCA Crim 2864) helpful:

'The court should take into account the nature of the current offence; the offender's history of offending including not just the kind of offence but its circumstances and the sentence passed ... and, whether the offending demonstrates any pattern; social and economic factors in relation to the offender including accommodation, employability, education, associates, relationships and drug or alcohol abuse; and the offender's thinking, attitude towards offending and supervision and emotional state. Information in relation to these matters will most readily, though not exclusively, come from antecedents and pre-sentence probation and medical reports. *The Guide for Sentence for Public Protection*, issued in June 2005 for the National Probation Service, affords valuable guidance for probation officers. The guidance in relation to assessment of dangerousness in para 5 is compatible with the terms of this judgment. The sentencer will be guided, but not bound by, the assessment of risk in such reports ...'

STATING REASONS FOR GRANTING BAIL

Where a court decides to grant bail to a defendant charged with any of the following five offences which are sentenceable by life imprisonment:

(i) murder or attempted murder;

(ii) manslaughter;

(iii) rape or attempted rape,

and the prosecution (as will almost certainly be the case) has made representations regarding the risk of failure to surrender, interference with witnesses or commission of an offence, the court 'shall state the reasons for its decision and shall cause those reasons to be included in the record of proceedings': BA 1976 Sch 1, Part 1, para. 9A. Note that in cases of this nature, the prosecution may seek to appeal against the bail decision under the provisions of the Bail (Amendment) Act 1993, which causes the defendant to remain in custody pending the appeal outcome.

MURDER: BAIL CONDITION TO UNDERGO MEDICAL EXAMINATION

If bail is granted where the defendant is charged with murder, not only must the court state its reasons but must also require reports on the accuser's mental condition.

BA 1976 s3

(6A) In the case of a person accused of murder the court granting bail shall, unless it considers that satisfactory reports on his mental condition have already been obtained, impose as conditions of bail –

    (a) a requirement that the accused shall undergo examination by two medical practitioners for the purpose of enabling such reports to be prepared; and

    (b) a requirement that he shall for that purpose attend such an institution or place as the court directs and comply with any other directions which may be given to him for that purpose by either of those practitioners.

One of the doctors must be approved for the purposes of MHA 1983, s12 (see Stone, 1995: 150): s3(6B).

If the defendant has previously been remanded in custody, reports may already have been undertaken or sought by a prison medical officer and it will often be in the defendant's interests for psychiatric reports to be obtained so that the possibility of a defence of diminished responsibility can be considered or the issue of fitness to plead can be explored (see Stone, 1995, Chapter 6).

In *R v Central Criminal Court, ex parte Porter* [1992] Crim LR 121, where magistrates had purported to grant bail in a murder case without imposing a s3(6A) condition, the Divisional Court ruled that this flawed order was a nullity. It was thus not open to the Crown Court judge to purport subsequently to vary the defendant's bail to include a requirement of psychiatric assessment. The original grant of bail should have been revoked and the defendant granted bail afresh with the proper statutory condition. The Divisional Court also indicated that the question of whether a medical report obtained under s3(6A) should be disclosed to the prosecution was a matter for the trial judge's discretion after reading the report (or, exceptionally, the discretion of another judge conducting a pre-trial review).

BAIL OFFENCES: INELIGIBILITY FOR BAIL IN CASES OF LIFE IMPRISONMENT

Partial implementation of ss 14 and 15(1) and (2) of the CJA 2003 in relation to offences with a maximum sentence of life imprisonment came into effect on 1 January 2007 *(Home Office Circular 039/2006)*. These provisions, which relate to court bail decisions only and do not apply to police bail decisions, introduce a change to the test for the court to apply when making a bail decision in circumstances where it appears to the court that the defendant has committed the offence while on bail in other criminal proceedings, or where the defendant has previously failed to surrender to bail during the proceedings.

Section 14(1) substitutes a new para. 2A of Part 1 of Sch 1 to the 1976 Bail Act. This provides that if a defendant over 18 years of age appears to have committed the offence whilst on bail in criminal proceedings, he (sic) may not be granted bail unless the court is satisfied that there is no significant risk of his committing an offence while on bail. This applies only where the offence for which bail is being considered is one for which the defendant is liable on conviction to a maximum sentence of life imprisonment. Section 14(2) provides that if a defendant is under 18 years of age and it appears that the offence was committed whilst on bail in criminal proceedings, the court should give particular weight to the fact that the defendant was on bail in criminal proceedings when determining whether there are substantial grounds for believing he would commit a further offence whilst on bail.

Section 15(1) substitutes a new para. 6 of Part 1 of Sch 1 of the 1976 Act. This provides that if a defendant 18 years or over, having been released on bail in or in connection with the proceedings for the offence, failed to surrender to custody he may not be granted bail unless the court is satisfied there is no significant risk that, if released on bail, he would fail to surrender to custody. Again, this only applies where the offence for which bail is being considered is one for which the defendant may, on conviction, receive a life sentence. Section

15(2) provides that if a defendant under 18 years of age – having been released on bail – failed to surrender to custody, the court should give particular weight to the fact of his failure to surrender.

PREVIOUS CONVICTIONS: INELIGIBILITY FOR BAIL

Bail cannot be granted to a person charged with or convicted of the following five 'life' offences:

(i)   murder or attempted murder;

(ii) manslaughter;

(iii) rape or attempted rape,

where the defendant has a previous conviction for any of the above offences (including the Scottish law offence of 'culpable homicide') and, in the case of a previous conviction for manslaughter or culpable homicide, received a custodial sentence. The past and present offences do not have to fall into the same category.

CJPOA 1994 s25

(1) A person who, in any proceedings, has been charged with or convicted of an offence to which this section applies in circumstances to which it applies shall not be granted bail in those proceedings.

(2) Lists the five offences, above (i)–(iii).

(3) This section applies to a person charged with, or convicted of, any such offence only if he has been previously convicted by or before a court in any part of the UK of any such offence or of culpable homicide, and if he was then sentenced to imprisonment or, if he was then a child or young person, to long-term detention under any of the relevant enactments.

This measure removing the court's discretion in such cases was introduced as part of a wider policy of tightening up on bail. Bail would have been refused in many cases of this nature under the previous law but this later provision applies no matter how long ago the previous conviction arose and could impact in a somewhat draconian way. The provision applies whether or not an appeal is pending against the earlier conviction or sentence (s25(4)).

REDUCTION IN SENTENCE FOR A GUILTY PLEA

Section 144 of the CJA 2003 provides:

> "In determining what sentence to pass on an offender who has pleaded guilty to an offence in proceedings before that or another court, a court must take into account –

(a) the stage in the proceedings for the offence at which the offender indicated his intention to plead guilty, and

(b) the circumstances in which the indication is given."

Where the court determines that there should be a whole life minimum term imposed, there will be no reduction for a guilty plea. In such cases however, the court should take into consideration the fact that the offender has pleaded guilty to murder when deciding whether a whole life sentence is appropriate. That is the exception. In other cases of murder, the provisions contained within s144 apply. However, as the Sentencing Guidelines Council point out, there are significant differences between the usual fixed term sentence and the minimum term (or tariff) set following the imposition by the court of a mandatory life sentence:

'The most significant of these, from the sentencer's point of view, is that a reduction for a plea of guilty in the case of murder will have double the effect on time served in custody when compared with a determinate sentence. This is because a determinate sentence will provide (in most circumstances) for the release of the offender on licence half way through the total sentence whereas in the case of murder a minimum term is the period in custody before consideration is given by the Parole Board to whether release is appropriate.'

(Sentencing Guidelines Council, 2007, page 8).

In reaching a decision regarding a reduction in sentence for a guilty plea, the court has to consider several factors, detailed below.

1. It has to weigh carefully the overall length of the minimum term, taking into consideration other reductions for which the offender may be eligible thereby avoiding a combination which leads to an inappropriately short sentence.

2. Where the minimum term is reduced, the sentence will not exceed one-sixth or 5 years.

3. The court has to apply the 'sliding scale' of reduction from a maximum of one-sixth or 5 years only in cases where a guilty plea has been entered at the first reasonable opportunity, with a recommended 5% for a late guilty plea.

4. Having taken the above into account, the court should then ensure the minimum term accurately reflects the seriousness of the offence.

The process for calculating a reduction in sentence for a plea of guilty in relation to discretionary life sentences or Imprisonment for Public Protection (IPP) differs from the above. In these cases, calculation of a reduction in sentence follows the same formula that applies to determinate sentence offenders and the level of reduction should be a proportion of the total sentence imposed.

3
SENTENCING TO LIFE

MANDATORY LIFE SENTENCES

A life sentence must be imposed in the following three instances, all upon conviction of murder:

(i) *Life imprisonment* for a person aged 21 or over upon conviction, subject to (iii) (below): M(ADP)A 1965 s1(1).

(ii) *Custody for life* for a person under the age of 21 upon conviction, subject to (iii) below: CJA 1982 s8(1).

(iii) *Detention during Her Majesty's Pleasure* where a person convicted of murder 'appears to the court to have been under the age of 18 years at the time the offence was committed': CYPA 1933 s53(1). Note that the offender's age upon conviction is not the material factor in determining that this is the appropriate form of life sentence.

Many prosecutions which are initiated upon a charge of murder lead to a conviction for manslaughter, particularly on the basis of diminished responsibility under HA 1957 s2(1), a partial defence which cannot provide the basis of the initial charge and must originate from a murder indictment. The prosecution may be willing to accept such a reduced plea on grounds of substantially impaired responsibility (see Stone, 1995) but should only do so where there is clear evidence of 'mental imbalance'. Ultimately, the judge must determine whether the lesser plea should be accepted and may, in exceptional cases, require that there should be a trial of the murder charge before a jury.

Recommendation of Minimum Period in Custody
M(ADP)A 1965 s1(2)

On sentencing any person convicted of murder to imprisonment for life the Court may at the same time declare the period which it recommends to the Secretary of State as the minimum period which in its view should elapse before the Secretary of State orders the release of that person on licence ...

Scope to make a recommendation in open court at the time of passing sentence of *life imprisonment* (but not *custody for life* or s53(1) detention) is an optional power rather than a requirement and, as will be explored in Chapter 7, is of persuasive rather than binding weight. As such it is not part of the sentence nor an order of the Court and is not open to appeal: *R v Aitken* [1966] 1 WLR 1076 and *R v Bowden* (1983) 77 Cr App R 66. This was reiterated recently in

R v Leaney [1995] Crim LR 669 where the Court of Appeal, headed by the Lord Chief Justice, clearly felt that the circumstances of the killing (a racially motivated stabbing of a black student after a minor street incident) did not merit a 20 year recommendation and called on the Government to reconsider the law relating to mandatory life sentencing and to avoid 'anomalous distinctions' between the treatment of mandatory and discretionary lifers. Opportunity for such reconsideration came in June 1995 when an amendment to the Criminal Appeal Bill, giving right of appeal, was successfully moved in the House of Lords but the Government subsequently caused this to be rejected in the Commons.

Any recommendation should not be for a period of less than 12 years: *R v Flemming* [1973] 57 Cr App R 524, disapproving of a recommended minimum term of ten years but without explanation of the Court's reasoning. In very exceptional cases, the judge may recommend that the defendant is never released. Because *Flemming* implied that recommendations should only be made in cases of considerable gravity, the practice has since been adopted very infrequently. The House of Lords Select Committee on Murder and Life Imprisonment (1989, para. 147) noted that between January 1966 and June 1989 minimum recommendations had been made in only about 270 cases (9%) out of 2,927 life sentences for murder passed during that period. Padfield (1995) suggested that the Lord Chief Justice should issue a Practice Statement encouraging trial judges to make recommendations so that tariff periods may be discussed routinely in open court.

Questionable Rationale

According to the Committee on the Penalty for Homicide chaired by former Lord Chief Justice Lane (1993), the mandatory life sentence for murder 'is founded on the assumption that murder is a crime of such unique heinousness that the offender forfeits for the rest of his existence his right to be set free'. The Committee declared this assumption a fallacy, because the definition of murder embraces a wide range of acts of homicide many of which are not 'truly heinous' or 'really wicked'.

> 'It is logically and jurisprudentially wrong to require judges to sentence all categories of murderer in the same way, regardless of the particular circumstances of the case before them.'

Following the lead of the House of Lords Select Committee on Murder and Life Imprisonment (1989) and the unsuccessful efforts of former Lord Chancellor Lord Hailsham and other distinguished jurists to amend the law at the time of the passage of the CJA 1991, the Committee recommended that the trial judge should be enabled to pass such sentence as is merited by the facts of the case, whether a determinate term of imprisonment or a hospital order, reserving life imprisonment for the most serious or dangerous offenders. This would reduce the resort to 'unsavoury' evasive devices such as pleas of diminished responsibility, would provide more certainty for prisoners and would enable the Prison Service to devote more resources to prisoners serving long determinate sentences who may well present a greater risk to society than the average lifer currently.

Despite the weight of evidence it received favouring the abolition of the mandatory life sentence, the House of Commons Home Affairs Committee (1995) recommended that the mandatory sentence should stay, albeit concluding that the current role of the Home Secretary in determining release should end. The Committee felt that abolition would imply a down-grading in the severity with which society views the crime of murder and argued that the mandatory sentence meets concern for public safety. At the same time it was keen to make the tariff-setting procedure more open, so that the public should better understand the link between the gravity of the crime and the length of periods spent in custody. It thus reached the preliminary conclusion that the trial judge should declare the tariff period in open court, that this should be open to appeal by prosecution and defence and that the issue of release after tariff expiry should be assessed by a Parole Board panel. In its final report, the Committee confirmed its preliminary proposals (see page 5).

Use of Mandatory Life Sentencing

In the five years 1989–1993 (figures for 1994 being provisional and incomplete), 3,294 defendants were indicted for murder, of whom 2,376 (72%) were convicted of homicide, 1,010 (31%) for murder, 362 for manslaughter (diminished responsibility), 984 for manslaughter (other) and 20 for infanticide.

In the five years 1990–1994, 966 persons received a mandatory life sentence, 805 (83%) being aged 21 or over and only 51 (5%) being female:

	Life Imprisonment	Custody for Life	s53(1)
Male	766	83	66
Female	39	6	6

Source: Supplementary Criminal Statistics for England and Wales

Juvenile Offenders

The number of children and young persons convicted of murder has remained relatively small and reasonably consistent in recent years, though subject to a predictable increase from 1993 when 17-year-olds were brought within the ambit of CYPA 1933 s53(1). Of the 72 defendants sentenced to detention during Her Majesty's pleasure in the period 1990–1994, only four were aged under 14, two males in 1993 and 1994 respectively. Between 1963 and 1994, only ten children aged 10–13 were convicted of murder in England and Wales (Parliamentary written answer 25 April 1996). Despite these very small numbers, the trial in 1994 of the two 11-year-old boys convicted of the murder of James Bulger attracted considerable debate about the appropriate treatment of children who face prosecution for homicide. The public setting and surrounding media interest, the procedural formality, ceremony and separation of defendants in the dock from their legal representative, the delay arising from the organisation of a jury trial and the intimidatory demands and atmosphere facing a jury of 12 adults, all combine to place children at a disadvantage. Can they be expected to function properly, to understand proceedings, to give full instructions to their lawyer, to give full evidence? A seminar of experts convened by 'Justice' (1996a) were agreed 'that it was positively harmful to try children in adult courts and that understanding the proceedings was often the beginning of treatment'.

'Justice' has recommended that children under 14 should not be liable for public trial in adult criminal courts but should be tried in private, so that their identities are protected and only the facts of the case and the sentence are made public, before a special panel of a judge and two magistrates with relevant experience and training. 'Justice' also proposes that for defendants under 18 the distinction between murder and manslaughter should not apply and that they should face a single offence of homicide so that, instead of concentrating on the difficult notion of intent, the more important judicial task would be to determine the most appropriate sentence in each case, with a view to the protection of society and the young person's rehabilitation. There would no longer be a mandatory sentence but discretion to impose the appropriate sentence, including indefinite custody in certain cases. The nature of the regime for indeterminate detention and the basis for decisions for release under such a revised sentencing system for juveniles are addressed in Chapters 4 and 7.

DISCRETIONARY LIFE SENTENCES

A discretionary life sentence arises in the following three instances where a person is convicted of an offence for which an adult could receive a maximum term of life imprisonment:

(i) Life imprisonment for a person aged 21 or over upon conviction.

(ii) Custody for life for a person aged 18 or over but under the age of 21 upon conviction: CJA 1982 s8(2).

(iii) Detention under CYPA 1933 s53(2) and (3) for a person aged at least 10 but not more than 17 upon conviction.

Though life remains the maximum sentence for over 50 offences, many are seldom subject to prosecution. The more common offences carrying life sentences are as follows:

Homicide, Violence and other Offences against the Person: manslaughter, infanticide, child destruction, attempted murder, soliciting to murder, wounding or grievous bodily harm with intent (s18), kidnapping, false imprisonment, torture, assault with intent to rob.

Sexual Offences: rape, sexual intercourse or incest with a girl aged under 13, buggery upon a boy aged under 16, a woman or an animal.

Offences against Property: robbery, arson, criminal damage with intent to endanger life, aggravated burglary.

Drug Offences: production, supply or possession with intent to supply a Class A drug.

Firearms Offences: possession of firearms with intent to endanger life or injure property, use of firearms to resist arrest, carrying firearms with intent to commit an indictable offence.

Offences against Justice: perverting the course of justice, escaping from lawful custody.

Criminal Justice Act 2003, Sections 225–6

There is a statutory requirement for this sentence to be imposed in cases where the court considers the gravity of the offence justifies it.

'The Most Exceptional Circumstances'

'Life imprisonment ... must only be passed in the most exceptional circumstances': Lord Lane CJ in *R v Wilkinson* (1983) 5 Cr App R(S) 105. The leading guideline case, prior to CJA 1991, on the appropriate use of discretionary life imprisonment, *R v Hodgson* (1968) 52 Cr App R 113, reiterated by *Wilkinson*, indicated that a life term will be justified only where three criteria are satisfied:

(i) *Gravity*: the offence or offences are in themselves grave enough to require a very long sentence.

(ii) *Instability*: it appears from the nature of the offences, or from the offender's history, that s/he is a person of mental instability who, if at liberty, would probably re-offend and present a grave danger to the public.

(iii) *Danger*: the offender will remain unstable and present a potential danger of especially serious consequences to others for a long time and/or an uncertain period of time.

The *Hodgson* criteria clearly suggest that a discretionary life sentence will be imposed as a protective measure to avoid risk to the public, *ie* as a longer sentence than commensurate with the seriousness of the current offence.

The judiciary have been properly conscious of the psychological impact of indeterminacy. In *R v Zacharcko* (1988) 10 Cr App R(S) 116, Lord Lane CJ acknowledged that a life term 'imposes great strain upon the person ... because of the uncertainty ... So if possible the judge will, when s/he can, impose a determinate sentence'.

Former Lord Chief Justice, Lord Bingham, ruled that the *Hodgson* criteria can be re-stated as two heads (*R v Whittaker* (1996) *The Times*, 24 July):

(i)   the offender has been convicted of a very serious offence;

(ii) there are good grounds for believing that the offender may remain a serious danger to the public for a period which cannot be reliably estimated at the date of sentence.

Passing a discretionary life sentence upon the defendant Whittaker who was already subject to a mandatory life sentence and had caused grievous bodily harm with intent whilst on temporary licence, in place of a determinate term, on application by the Attorney General, the Court of Appeal made clear that though evidence of an offender's mental state is highly relevant, the trial judge had been wrong to rule out the possibility of imposing discretionary life because there was no medical evidence of personality disorder or mental instability. There was sufficient basis to conclude that the offender was likely to represent a serious danger to the public for an indeterminate time.

Rape: Specific Guidance

The Court of Appeal has not developed the generic *Hodgson* criteria in the context of specific crimes except in regard to rape. In *R v Billam* [1986] 1 WLR 349, the leading guideline case for this offence, Lord Lane CJ advised:

'Where the defendant's behaviour has manifested perverted or psychopathic tendencies or gross personality disorder, and where he is likely, if at large, to remain a danger to women for an indefinite time, a life sentence will not be inappropriate.'

In reality, this adds little or nothing to the basic principles of life sentencing.

POST-SENTENCE REPORT BY PROBATION OFFICER

The home probation officer is required to prepare a report as soon as possible following sentence and within four months, to provide 'information that will be of value in the care and management of the life sentence prisoner and the preparation of the Life Sentence Plan, and will be additional to what is contained in any report to the court'. The report should outline the circumstances of the offence and should include:

(i)   evidence of patterns of offending behaviour which preceded or precipitated the offence;

(ii)   any history or evidence of drug or alcohol misuse;

(iii)   advice on the assessment of the risk of re-offending or being a danger to the public;

(iv)   details of the significant persons whose relationships with the prisoner are affected by the crime and sentence.

(v)   In respect of these, what changes are apparent in their attitudes to the offender? How are these related to the offence of which he or she is now convicted?

(vi)   What are the chances of sustaining the relationship in a helpful way over a long period?

(vii)   Details of any practical problems at the prisoner's home, *eg* debts or loss of contribution to the household.

(viii)   Who can visit and with what degree of difficulty? Who cannot visit and who will not visit?

(ix)   What other consequences have flowed from events? *eg* if a man or woman has killed a partner, who is now looking after the children?

(x)   What hostility will the prisoner still have to face? *eg* family rejection, local feeling.

(xi)   What hostility do the prisoner's family have to face from neighbours, relatives of victim, etc.?

(xii)   How can the family together or individually be helped with their feelings about the offence, the offender, the sentence?

(xiii)   Is there anything of significance in the offender's medical history?

(xiv)   Particularly for younger lifers, what are their educational attainments and aspirations?

Report writers should be aware that this report will form part of the dossier at the time of formal review, and thus will be available to the prisoner. Copies should be sent to: the home area Chief Probation Officer; Parole and Lifer Group at Prison Service HQ; the governor and the seconded probation officer at the prison where the lifer is held.

APPEALS

As a defendant convicted and sentenced by the Crown Court, a person given a life sentence can appeal to the Court of Appeal (Criminal Division) (referred to hereafter as the Court) against *conviction, sentence* or both, save that no appeal lies against mandatory life sentence for murder which is a sentence fixed by law (CCA 1968 s9(1)). Given the legal complexity of the statutory provisions regulating appeal, it is possible to give only an outline of the appeals process and grounds for appeal.

Appeal against Sentence

Appeal against a discretionary life sentence (or against the specified 'relevant part' under CJA 1991 s34) may proceed only if either the judge passing sentence has granted a certificate that the case is fit for such an appeal or, more usually, the offender has been granted leave to appeal by the Court of Appeal (CAA 1968 s11). The defendant must file their notice of application for leave within 28 days of sentence. The application is normally considered by a single judge after consideration of the papers. If the single judge refuses the application, the defendant may apply to the Court but must normally serve notice of intent to renew the application within 14 days of receiving notification from the Court's Registrar of refusal of leave. Legal Aid is available for advice on whether it is worth renewing an initially unsuccessful application but does not cover representation before the Court at the renewed application.

If leave to appeal is granted, the appeal is heard by the Court consisting of three judges, presided over either by the Lord Chief Justice or a Lord Justice of Appeal sitting usually with two High Court judges. The most frequent basis of an appeal against sentence is that the sentence is 'wrong in principle or manifestly excessive', non-statutory phrasing which reflects the Court's general approach. A lifer appellant may thus seek to demonstrate that the *Hodgson* criteria were not fulfilled in their case or, even if accepting that a life sentence was appropriate, that the 'relevant part' specified under s34 fell outside the appropriate range for a determinate sentence for the crime in question.

Note that if a defendant appeals against a determinate sentence of imprisonment, the Court may not substitute a life sentence (*R v Whittaker* [1967] Crim LR 431).

Appeal against Conviction

Appeal against conviction for murder or an offence attracting a discretionary life sentence may be on a question of law, of fact or both. Under the original provisions of CAA 1968 s1, a defendant has had a right of appeal where the ground is one of law alone but, under the provisions of CAA 1995 s1, all appeals will require leave to appeal unless the trial judge has certified that the case is fit for appeal. Leave to appeal is sought in the same way and subject to the same time limit (28 days running from date of conviction) as in respect of an appeal against sentence (above). The Royal Commission on Criminal Justice

(1993) recommended that the Court of Appeal should be more prepared to overturn verdicts which it believes are or may be unsafe and to order retrials where practicable, and to receive fresh evidence and to accept alleged errors by trial lawyers as a ground of appeal. It remains to be seen whether the rewording of the Court's statutory powers introduced by the 1995 Act will liberalise the Court's past somewhat over-sceptical approach. A prisoner embarking on an appeal may seek to weigh whether a lengthy appeal bid may affect their prospects of release; in the prominently publicised case of Emma Humphries, appealing against conviction for murder of her violent lover ten years after her life sentence, it was strongly suspected that she might have been released on life licence after completing her eight year tariff if she had accepted the murder verdict.

The original provision of CAA 1968, s2, has empowered the Court to allow the appeal on one of three grounds:

(i) conviction unsafe or unsatisfactory;

(ii) wrong decision on any question of law;

(iii) material irregularity in the course of trial;

subject to a proviso that the Court may nevertheless dismiss the appeal if it considers that no miscarriage of justice has actually occurred. CAA 1995 s2 substitutes a single basis for allowing an appeal, ie that the Court thinks that the conviction is 'unsafe'. The test is clearly subjective, requiring the Court to consider whether it is content to let the matter stand as it is or whether 'there is some lurking doubt' which makes the appeal judges 'wonder whether an injustice has been done' (R v Cooper [1969] 1 QB 267).

Appeal Following Guilty Plea

Though the Court is rarely prepared to grant leave to appeal if the applicant pleaded guilty at Crown Court, the Court may be willing to allow an appeal despite this consideration if it appears that the defendant did not appreciate the nature of the charge or did not intend to admit that s/he was guilty of it, or upon the admitted facts s/he could not in law have been convicted of the offence charged. Further, in very exceptional circumstances the applicant may be permitted to appeal even though s/he knew what s/he was doing, intended to make the plea entered and pleaded guilty without equivocation, if it nevertheless appears that the conviction is unsafe. Thus in R v Lee [1984] 1 WLR 578, the appellant's convictions for several offences of arson and manslaughter were quashed because (a) fresh evidence had come to light strongly suggesting that he could not have committed at least some of the crimes, (b) his confessions to the police were unreliable because of his low intelligence and the possibility that he confessed because of a desire for notoriety and (c) his plea was influenced by the knowledge that a bed had been obtained for him at a psychiatric hospital and he hoped he would receive a hospital order if he admitted the offences. His legal representatives had been anticipating a not guilty plea.

Fresh Evidence

The Court has wide power to receive further evidence if it appears that this is 'likely to be credible' (CAA 1968 s23, reworded as 'capable of belief' by CAA 1995 s4) and the Court is satisfied that there is a reasonable explanation for the failure to adduce it at trial. Thus in *R v Lattimore* (1975) 62 Cr App R 53, the appellants had been convicted of murder and arson, the prosecution evidence indicating that they had strangled their victim and set fire to his house with his body inside it. The case was established largely on the strength of confession evidence which was unsuccessfully challenged at the trial on grounds of the defendants' young age and limited intelligence and the pressure placed upon them in police interview. On appeal, the defence successfully introduced further scientific and medical evidence that several hours elapsed between the victim's death and the house fire, contrary to the confessions which indicated that the arson had been committed immediately after the killing.

The fresh evidence may suggest that the defendant had a partial defence to murder. In *R v Ahluwalia* [1992] 4 All ER 889, the appellant had killed her husband after many years of violence and abuse by throwing petrol into his bedroom and setting it alight. Her claims when tried for murder that she did not intend to kill him or cause him serious harm and that she acted under provocation were unsuccessful. On her appeal, a psychiatric report available at the trial but somehow overlooked expressed the opinion that she was suffering a major depressive disorder and thus suggesting diminished responsibility. Though the Court of Appeal indicated that 'this Court would require much persuasion to allow such a defence to be raised for the first time here if the option had been exercised at the trial not to pursue it', in this unusual instance it was considered in the interests of justice to admit the further evidence. The Court noted:

> 'If there is no evidence to support diminished responsibility at the time of the trial, this Court would view wholly retrospective medical evidence obtained long after the trial with considerable scepticism.'

Power to Order Re-Trial

Though the normal consequence of a successful appeal is the quashing of the conviction, so that the appellant cannot be re-tried either for the offence in respect of which the appeal was brought, or for any other offence of which s/he could have been convicted through an alternative verdict, CAA 1968 s7 gives the Court a general discretion to order a re-trial, where this appears to be required in the interests of justice. This was ordered in *Ahluwalia* (above) to allow proper consideration of the claim of diminished responsibility. The well-known case of Sara Thornton provides a prominent example of re-trial, the defendant being bailed pending her second trial for murder of her husband.

Substitution of Verdict

Under CAA 1968 s3, the Court may substitute for the verdict found by the jury a verdict of guilty of another offence and impose an alternative sentence in substitution for the sentence passed at the trial, provided that the Court is satisfied that the jury must have been satisfied of facts which proved the defendant guilty of the other offence. Thus, in the context of life sentence crime, in *R v Spratt* [1980] 1 WLR 554 where the defendant had been convicted of murder, the Court took account of further evidence which did not negate his unlawful killing but which suggested his diminished responsibility at the time. The Court was thus able to substitute a verdict of guilty of manslaughter.

The Criminal Cases Review Commission

Under CAA 1968 s17, the Home Secretary has had power at any time to refer to the Court of Appeal the case of a person convicted on indictment, 'if he thinks fit'. The Minister is advised by the Mental Health and Criminal Cases Unit at the Home Office. Such a reference must be made either following an application by the convicted person or on the Home Secretary's initiative. The whole case could be referred, in which case it would be treated as an appeal, or merely some point arising in the case on which the Court would give an opinion. This power to intervene in cases of possible miscarriage of justice, where appeal rights have been exhausted, has been used sparingly, involving approximately 10 to 12 cases yearly. The Royal Commission on Criminal Justice (1993) considered that the Home Office had neither the necessary commitment nor the resources to undertake the role more proactively and proposed a new review body which would be better resourced and independent of the executive. In a recent prominent instance of this power, the Home Secretary referred the case of the 'Bridgewater Four', 18 years after the crime, in the light of a fresh investigation by another police force and a Divisional Court judgment ordering the Home Secretary to disclose the information arising from that investigation to the defence. The Criminal Cases Review Commission (CCRC) was set up under the Criminal Appeal Act 1995 to investigate suspected miscarriages of justice. Before referring a conviction or sentence to the Court of Appeal, the Commission must consider 'that there is a real possibility that conviction, verdict, finding or sentence would not be upheld were the reference to be made' (CAA 1995 s13(1)(a)). This must be because of an argument or evidence not raised at trial or on appeal (s13(1)(b)) and an appeal in the normal way must have been heard or leave to appeal refused (s13(1)(c)). However, the CCRC may still refer the case 'where there are exceptional circumstances for making it', even though the criteria of s13(1)(b) and (c) are not fulfilled (s13(2)). Where the Commission decides not to refer a case, it is required to give a statement of its reasons to the applicant. Though the Royal Commission argued that there should be legal aid to convicted persons to cover advice and assistance in making representations to the CCRC, the 1995 Act does not make provision of this nature. Assessing the likely impact of the CCRC's work, Malleson (1995) concluded:

> 'The most likely benefits of the establishment of the Criminal Cases Review Commission will be an improvement in the treatment of cases which have fresh evidence to put before the Commission. With greater resources, more staff and a better relationship with the Court of Appeal, the Commission is likely to offer a much improved service in such cases by ensuring that they are more fully investigated. If the Court interprets the phrase 'capable of belief' as representing even a slight liberalisation of its approach to fresh evidence there is also more chance that such cases will result in the conviction being quashed. The losers may be those cases which fall outside this narrow category, particularly the small number of cases which are based solely on the ground that the evidence before the jury was weak and verdict was wrong, or where the fresh evidence is limited or might only be revealed after more extensive investigations. These cases are likely to cause the Commission the most difficulties. If it sees that their chances of success on referral are slim it may be unlikely to invest time and resources in them. Their merits may not be tested and they may continue to fall through the safety net of the review process.'

By the end of September 2006, CCRC had dealt with over 9,000 applications – of these, 291 had been heard by the Court of Appeal resulting in 199 cases being quashed, 89 upheld and 3 reserved.

Royal Prerogative of Mercy

In very occasional circumstances of miscarriage of justice, the Court of Appeal may be bypassed and the convicted person can receive a 'free pardon', granted by the Crown on the advice of the Home Secretary who in turn is advised by the Mental Health and/or the Criminal Cases Review Commission. The effect is not to quash the conviction but to release the recipient from 'all pains, penalties and punishments whatsoever that may ensue from their conviction'. According to the CCRC's Annual Report, the Home Secretary's power, under section 16 of the Act, to seek the Commission's advice in relation to recommendations concerning the prerogative of mercy has never been used; nor has the Commission exercised its power under the same section to make any such recommendations to the Home Secretary (CCRC Annual Report, 2006/2007).

Redress

Lawyers acting for persons who have spent lengthy periods subject to life sentence before release after a successful appeal against conviction will normally seek financial compensation for their clients from the Home Office. The enormous psychological impact of such experience has recently begun to receive clinical attention but so far little or no counselling and treatment has been made available for individuals who have been emotionally damaged by miscarriages of justice.

AUTOMATIC LIFE SENTENCE

The automatic life sentence – better known perhaps as the 'two strikes and out' legislation – was enacted in October 1998 as part of the Crime (Sentences) Act 1997. Automatic life sentence was handed on the conviction of a second 'serious' offence by the defendant who must have been over 18 years of age at the time of conviction, not commission of the offence.

Qualifying Offences

Violent Offences

Includes attempted murder, threat or conspiracy to murder, manslaughter, wounding with intent to inflict grievous bodily harm, robbery involving use of firearms, possession of a firearm with intent to endanger life or to commit an indictable offence or to resist arrest.

Sexual Offences

Includes rape, attempted rape, unlawful sexual intercourse with a girl under 13.

The automatic life sentence ceased to become a sentencing option in April 2005 when the sentence for indeterminate public protection came into being.

INDETERMINATE SENTENCES FOR PUBLIC PROTECTION (IPP)

Under s225 of the Criminal Justice Act 2003, there is provision for sentencing offenders to an indeterminate sentence of imprisonment for public protection. The IPP sentence applies only to offences that were committed on or after 4 April 2005. The court is required to pass this sentence in cases where the offence is specified under Sch 15 of the Act and the court believes the defendant to pose a danger to the public. The tariff is set at the time of sentence and reflects the standard determinate sentence that the person would have received had they not fulfilled the criteria of 'dangerousness', under Chapter 5 of the Act. The length of the sentence is then halved, since determinate sentenced prisoners, sentenced under the CJA 2003, are automatically released at the halfway stage. Time spent on remand is also subtracted.

In all IPP cases the Parole Board can, where it deems it to be appropriate, direct that the length of the licence shall cease to have effect after a period of ten years. Between April 2005 and October 2006, 1,000 offenders had been sentenced to IPP causing Christine Glenn, Chief Executive of the Parole Board, to remark, 'The use of these sentences by the courts has been even greater than expected' (*Parole Board Annual Report* 05/06). The Lord Chief Justice, Lord Phillips, is reported to have warned the All-Party Parliamentary Penal Affairs Group that such sentences are being imposed for 'comparatively trivial offences' (*The Observer*, 18 June 2006). The Howard League For Penal Reform has also weighed into the debate, opposing IPP as a matter of principle whilst at the same time arguing that if the sentence is to remain on the statute books, it should only be used in exceptional circumstances (Howard League, 2007).

Arguably, the process of dealing with dangerous offenders and the interpretation of 'dangerousness' has proved to be one of the most problematical areas of the CJA 2003.

The process for adults is as follows.

Stage 1

Is the present offence a specified one? (A specified offence is one of the 153 offences listed in Sch 15 of the Act.) If so, 'dangerousness' must be considered and has to be addressed, whether or not the defendant has a previous conviction for a relevant offence.

Stage 2

If the court finds danger then, unless the requirements of the Mental Health Act 1983 allow a hospital order to be made, the court has to impose one of three sentences:

(i)   life imprisonment;

(ii) imprisonment for public protection;

(ii) an extended sentence.

If danger is not found then life imprisonment for public protection and an extended sentence are not available.

Stage 3

If the present offence is a specified offence but not a serious offence then the sentence has to be an extended sentence. If the present offence is a serious offence (defined as carrying a possible maximum sentence of ten years or more, including life) then the sentence has to be one of life imprisonment if the offence carries a possible life sentence and if a life sentence is justified. If a life sentence is not justified then it has to be imprisonment for public protection.

Stage 4

The court has to determine the period before which the defendant cannot be considered for parole and release on licence under s82A of the Act. Calculation of this period includes deciding what the ordinary discretionary prison sentence would have been, half that sentence less the time spent on remand in custody.

A number of cases in respect of the IPP cases have now been heard by the Court of Appeal (*R v Lang & Others* (2005), *R v ISA* (2006). As Stone (2006) notes, the Appeal Court expressed:

> 'sympathy for sentences faced with applying what it described as an 'astonishingly complex' labyrinth of measures, the Court sought to offer general guidance, particularly in respect of the critical statutory test, namely whether the offender poses a 'significant risk' to members of the public by the commission of further specified offences. This issue is further amplified by an assumption (contained in s229) of dangerousness in relation to adults with a prior conviction for a specified offence, rebuttable only if the court can conclude that this is an unreasonable conclusion.'

EXTENDED SENTENCES

Provision is made under the CJA 2003 for extended sentences (ss 227, 228 and 247). The sentence consists of a custodial term plus an extended period on supervision. The custodial element of the sentence has to be for at least 12 months. Release can be obtained on approval of the Parole Board from the halfway stage onwards to the end of the custodial period. Supervision by the Probation Service will be until the sentence expiry date.

4
LIFERS IN THE PRISON SYSTEM

THE LIFER POPULATION

The lifer population in the United Kingdom has risen inexorably over the last 50 years, and is set to continue to rise at a more rapid rate than previously because of the advent of IPP. At the time when the Homicide Act 1957 (which curtailed the death penalty) was passed, there were 133 lifers in custody. In 1996, 3,517 prisoners (including those recalled from licence) were serving life sentences in England and Wales. By 31 October 2003, this had risen to 5,445: of which 5,305 were men, 170 women and 151 were young offenders. Nearly one in five of these life sentence prisoners were from minority ethnic groups. These figures led the Prison Reform Trust to label England and Wales as 'Europe's Lifer Capital'. Further to this, in 2004, they reported that England and Wales 'has more life sentence prisoners than all of the member states of the EU combined and has the highest number in the whole of Europe'.

On 31 July 2007, 9,659 prisoners were serving indeterminate sentences: of which 6,558 were lifers and 3,101 were serving a sentence of IPP. Of these, 9,351 were men and 308 were women and 705 were young offenders. At this time, 1,640 life licensees were under active supervision by the Probation Service.

LOCATION AND MANAGEMENT OF LIFERS

The responsibility for the management, release and recall of lifers and IPP prisoners lies collectively with the National Offender Management Service (NOMS), HM Prison Service, the National Probation Service, Independent Parole Board and the Lifer Review & Recall Section (LRRS). In an important step signifying the closer working relationship between prisons and probation services, the LRRS joined the National Offender Manager's Directorate on 1 April 2005 and now forms part of the Public Protection and Licensed Release Unit. Once sentenced, lifer prisoners will nearly always be returned to a local prison where they will remain to await a vacancy in a First Stage Lifer Prison. Ideally, this wait should not extend beyond four to six months, but prison population pressures may not facilitate such a move in the desired timescale. There are five First Stage prisons suitable only for Cat. A (High Risk) prisoners and these are Frankland, Full Sutton, Long Lartin, Wakefield and Dartmoor. Other prisons not in the High Security estate but offering First Stage facilities are Bristol, Cardiff, Dovegate Main, Gartree, Liverpool, Manchester, Swaleside and Wormwood Scrubs. There are four First Stage establishments for women at Buckley Hall, Bulwood Hall, Durham and Holloway (where women who require full-time medical care are likely to be located). First Stage prisons for Young Offenders can be found at Aylesbury, on the Oswald Unit at Castington and the Carlford Unit at Hollesley Bay. Young lifers must be transferred to an adult prison before their 22nd birthday. A newly-sentenced lifer can expect to spend anything from 18 months upwards in a First Stage prison, although this may be reduced for some prisoners with short tariffs or for those deemed to be making exceptionally good progress. Altogether there are now some 80 prisons offering services to life-sentenced prisoners.

Where appropriate, lifers should proceed to conditions of lower security and, until such time, will normally be held in Cat. B conditions (including IPPs), unless they are High Security prisoners of course. Because closed prisons provide a 'protective environment which is not appropriate to the problems facing a lifer on release and prison behaviour in conditions of freedom, it is in the community's interest, as well as that of individual lifers, that they be tested and assessed in a low security environment before release, and that pre-release preparation should be as thorough and varied as possible'. The aim is to ensure a progressive movement through the system, reflecting decreasing categories of security in line with the lifer's career and lifer sentence plan (see below). This principle is subject to two caveats:

- Because a number of lifers have in the past reached open and semi-open conditions inappropriately, when 'areas of concern' remained undressed, raising inappropriate expectations of release, the Lifer Management Unit 'will not progress lifers beyond Cat. B conditions unless they have addressed their offending behaviour' (Harris, 1991). (In a few instances, however, lifers may be transferred directly from a Main Centre to a Cat. C prison, bypassing Cat. B) Lifers who are considered to require SOTP training are now expected to undertake this before allocation to open conditions.

- A lifer will not be transferred to an open prison before the first formal review of their case by the Parole Board; and then only when a Home Office Minister or Senior Management in the Lifer Unit are satisfied that the criteria set out in the Home Secretary's Directions to the Parole Board have been met.

Where doubts might arise regarding a lifer's continued suitability for open conditions, or there are indications that the degree of potential risk to the public from the lifer is not acceptable, the Lifer Unit must be informed immediately and an open conditions review undertaken. Where a lifer absconds or is moved to another establishment for operational reasons, an open conditions failure report must be completed and sent to the Lifer Unit.

Life Sentence Plans

Life Sentence Plans (LSP) were introduced in 1993 for all lifers. They were revised in 2001 when the F75 reporting system was replaced. The purpose of the LSP is:

'to plan, monitor and record the means by which each lifer is supported in the process of achieving a reduction in risk during sentence such that he or she may safely be released on licence into the community at tariff expiry' (*LM* para 8.2).

The LSP will contain a detailed record of the index offence, summary of risk factors collated from whatever assessment systems have been used (Oasys, RM2000, SARA, etc.), offending behaviour targets and achievements, progress reviews and sentence planning objectives. From 7 January 2008, the LSP process will undergo a further revision. IPP sentenced prisoners will be managed by Offender Managers as part of Phase 3 of the offender management model. The remaining indeterminate prisoners, or more simply all those who are not serving an IPP sentence, will be managed by the prison Lifer Manager and will come into the scope of the OM model at a later date. However, the administrative process covering both IPP sentence prisoners and other lifers will be the same. I will outline briefly the processes and a more comprehensive list of the forms and associated timescales can be found in Appendix 3.

A post-sentence report needs to be completed by the OM. In cases where a PSR has been ordered, a brief report should be compiled using POST SRA. Where a PSR has not been ordered, a more in-depth report, POST SRB, needs to be completed. In both cases the report should be sent to the Pre-Release Section and the prison too, ready for the Initial Sentence Planning meeting. The prison-based Offender Supervisor (OS) completes the LISP IA within seven working days of sentence and forwards it to the OM and Pre-Release Section, who will open a file on the prisoner. The OS arranges the Initial Sentence Planning meeting and the Multi-Agency Risk Assessment Meeting (MARAM) which is recorded on LISP 1B with a copy forwarded to Pre-Release Section. Both meetings are chaired by the Offender Manager. Thereafter, sentence planning review meetings are arranged as appropriate by the Offender Manager.

The LSP should only be completed by trained staff within the Prison Service. The standard accredited training programme 'Life in the 21st Century' is no longer available due to the changes in lifer processes and a replacement training package has not yet been agreed at the time of writing. Whilst it is desirable that seconded staff should attend formal lifer training, *LM* para. 8.4 advises that LSP documentation can be completed by probation officers who have undertaken specific risk assessment training.

Source Sentence Planning Documents

Source Sentence Planning Documents replace the Confidential Memorandum. A copy is sent to the Governor of the Main Centre or other prison where the lifer is located by LRRS and is intended to assist staff in the preparation of their lifer reports at various stages during sentence. The document is prepared from a number of sources including police and probation reports, pre-trial medical reports, witness statements, trial transcripts, the trial judge's comments both in passing sentence and subsequently. It may contain matter which is unproven or uncorroborated but which is thought necessary to include in order to give a full and balanced account of the offence and the offender.

The supervising home probation officer as well as the prison probation officer will need to be aware of its contents and it is now possible for the home officer to obtain a copy on request from the prison or, in the event of difficulty, direct from LRRS. The document should not be disclosed to the lifer (or the lifer's family) by the probation officer. In a letter of guidance of 14 October 1992, the Home Office advised:

> 'If it becomes necessary for the supervising officer to confront the life sentence prisoner or life licensee with a difference between the lifer's version of events and the official version of what occurred, some general reference to, for example, 'the records of your case' should be made.'

Pending the completion of the Confidential Memorandum, PLRG will send the Governor a dossier of available information, known as the *confidential summary dossier*, as an interim source of information. It contains the police report, the pre-trial medical report, the pre-trial or post-sentence probation reports and the prisoner's antecedents/previous convictions. Preparation of the prisoner's Life Sentence Plan should not be undertaken until the dossier is received.

Male Young Offenders

Special Review Procedures apply to young offenders aged under 21 located in a young offender institution, detailed in *LM* para. 10.4. Shortly after reception and on completion of induction procedures, an initial review must consider the lifer's immediate needs, including their allocation to a wing or unit, and their work or education programme. After the first six months of settling in, a first internal review should be held to draw up a training plan addressing their personal, training and remedial needs, identifying areas of concern or risk and determining the options for dealing with them. This should be copied to Lifer Management Unit. Their second internal review, held six months later, must re-assess the training plan and give consideration to the age at which the young lifer should be transferred to the adult system. Transfer normally takes place between 21st and 22nd birthdays.

Sex Offender Treatment Programme

It is now clear policy to identify lifers at an early stage who should be assessed for SOTP and, where suitable, to undertake the programme before transfer to open conditions. Assessment centres for lifers are currently located in four prisons: Albany, Full Sutton, Maidstone and Wakefield. The normal criteria for identifying candidates for assessment are as follows:

- index offence includes a sexual offence; or

- index offence includes a sexual element (*eg* forensic evidence reveals bruising, wounding or biting of a sexual nature); or

- previous convictions include a sexual offence; or

- index offence shows behaviour which, if it persists, might lead to a sexual offence, *eg* a man murders someone as a consequence of their refusing to have sex with him.

Assessment spans two months and involves various individual interviews with SOTP staff, psychological tests and 'phallometric' testing with a penile plethysmograph (PPG). This test consists of a mercury-filled loop which is fitted around the subject's penis. The level of engorgement is measured as an indication of the degree of arousal in response to specific stimuli (see PRT, 1995).

The assessment follows the following stages:

1. Is sexual behaviour an area of concern?

2. If yes, has the prisoner the capacity to benefit from SOTP? (A prisoner will be considered unsuitable if he does not speak English, is of too low intelligence to understand the programme, is a substantial suicide risk, has a serious personality disorder or serious mental illness (or was suffering serious mental illness at the time of the offence).)

3. If yes, does the prisoner agree to participate? (If he does not agree, the assessment report would indicate that he could benefit from SOTP but is not yet motivated to do so. Lifers will thus realise that they will not achieve progress until they do participate.)

4. If yes, the factors which may have contributed to the prisoner's behaviour problems will be identified for specific attention in their programme.

The core programme runs for four months but for those who are considered to pose the greatest risk an extended programme is provided tackling problems of deviant sexual interests, difficulty in sustaining relationships, anger management, stress management and poor decision-making skills. A 'booster' programme is provided (currently at HMP Leyhill) shortly before release 'to reinforce gains made earlier and to develop relapse prevention strategies'.

Risk Assessment

The identification of risk factors and the monitoring of behaviour considered to be indicative of risk is now a crucial feature of lifer management and is considered by many LLOs to be their main professional function. Risk assessment remains a very imprecise discipline with considerable scope for personal bias and 'false positive' prediction, and particularly so with lifers, especially murderers, because their index offence is often their only instance of seriously violent behaviour.

A model of risk assessment initially adopted by psychologists at HMP Wakefield has tried to enhance risk assessment procedures, by seeking to identify the principal 'risk behaviours' ('risk factors') associated with the lifer's offence and using these to predict the types of similar behaviours which might be observed in prison. This then allows staff to focus more clearly on actual prison behaviour both as a clearer means of assessing the continuing risk posed by the prisoner and noting change over time, and also in determining which aspects of the prisoner's behaviours should be targeted for treatment intervention. A pilot study (McDougall and Clark, 1991; Clark *et al*, 1993) found that it is possible to predict offence-related prison behaviour on the basis of a behavioural analysis of lifers' previous offending with a reasonable degree of accuracy. Four clusters of prisoners were identified (1991):

Group A: 'disruptive, criminal element'
> *Offence Behaviour*: detailed planners, no loss of control, over-reaction to long-term events, blamed others. Had irrational beliefs and used a weapon premeditatively.

> *Prison Behaviour*: aggressive, disruptive, aloof, made many complaints, unable to see others' point of view, wouldn't accept decisions, no remorse for offence, changed associates, created exciting situations, manipulative of family/visitors. Hold grudges.

Group B: 'mainly sex offenders who try to present in a good light in prison'
> *Offence Behaviour*: detailed plans, motivation sexual or financial, used drug/alcohol disinhibitors, instrumental violence, but often no weapon. Antecedents were often marital or work problems or expectancies not met. Most likely to blame victim.

> *Prison Behaviour*: seek education, improving courses, very dependent on outside contact, attention seeker, seek help, manipulates the system, presents in a good light. Use pornography, present macho image, allow things to build up and tell lies.

Group C: 'more unstable type of murderers, with psychiatric problems'
> *Offence Behaviour*: murder spontaneous offence, involving loss of control and possibly sadistic attack, motivation is an over-reaction to immediate

events or an individual. The antecedents are lack of coping skills, being under stress and psychiatric problems.

Prison Behaviour: isolated, not involved in any activities, a poor worker whatever the job, makes threats to other inmates, refuses all help, tells lies, immature, enjoys observing violence.

Group D: 'domestic offenders'
Offence Behaviour: attacked relative, used an item that came to hand as a weapon spontaneously. Very remorseful afterwards.

Prison Behaviour: no hobbies, minimise offence, very remorseful, depressed, easily led, seeks a lot of support, positive attitude to staff, good worker.

The hope and belief is that patterns of problematic, risky behaviour in prison which might otherwise be overlooked or the significance swamped by otherwise unexceptional or insignificant behaviour will be tracked so that the continuing danger is realised and appropriate treatment offered.

This approach to risk assessment has now been absorbed throughout the lifer system and LLOs use an index of 'risk factors' together with a list of some 82 'prison behaviours'. For example, the risk factor 'hold grudges' is related to the following prison behaviours:

• grudges against staff, inmates or the system in general;

• over-controlled individual who remains calm most of the time but with occasional emotional outbursts when under stress;

• appears tense, unable to relax when on association or alone; shows other symptoms of stress;

• makes threats, either specific or general, against staff or other inmates;

• does not show any strong emotions, appears cold, detached from others on wing or in interviews.

As Mitchell (1992) warns, the majority of staff who help to shape the futures of lifers will have limited training or expertise in analysing and evaluating human behaviour and the subtleties of risk assessment may become somewhat blunted as efforts are made to absorb the new orthodoxy in a routine way. Some of the 'prison behaviours' listed may seem a little imprecise (*eg* 'conforms outwardly but may have underhand nature', associated with 'risk factor' of 'lacking empathy') and others lead to the undue pathologising of characteristics unsurprising for an indeterminate prisoner (*eg* 'over-controlled individual, remains calm most of the time but with occasional emotional outburst when under stress', associated with three 'risk factors': 'rigid views', 'unassertive' and 'cold and detached').

Penile Plethysmograph

The PPG test, now a standard procedure in the assessment of sex offenders (see page 41) is also used in the identification of offenders where it is suspected that there may be a latent sexual dimension to their index offence or their subsequent behaviour causes anxieties about their sexual predilections. Testing is undertaken in nine prisons: Albany, Dartmoor, Full Sutton, Leyhill, Maidstone, Swinfen Hall, Wakefield, Wandsworth and Whitemoor. Prisoners who do not fulfil any of the standard criteria prompting referral for SOTP assessment (see page 41) can be required to take the test if 'other factors' prompt uncertainty or anxiety in the course of risk assessment. A lifer may be referred on the prompting of the Parole Board who will refer the case to the Prison Service Psychology Unit. The process, the questionable reliability of the test, and the possible effects upon a prisoner of being tested inappropriately are detailed in a critical report by the Prison Reform Trust (1995).

An example of PPG testing, drawn to the present writer's attention, involved a lifer convicted of murder of a homosexual male victim, an offence denied throughout. On his recall from licence after being seen by police masturbating openly in a public toilet, behaviour considered unacceptably close to his index offence, the Parole Board determined that he should not be re-released because of 'the need to elucidate the nature of his psychosexual attitude'. PPG testing indicated that he was not aroused by homosexual stimuli and was thus not suitable for an SOTP course.

Transfers

Transfers are intended primarily to secure progressive movement through the system. It is important that lifers are given clear explanations about transfer decisions and do not build false hopes based on their progression to Cat. C or D conditions where they should realistically expect to be located for substantial periods. The principle of planned and purposeful change can appear arbitrary, illogical or frustrating in practice, even where transfers are intended to promote rehabilitative or therapeutic aims such as the opportunity to undertake SOTP. This can have adverse effects, particularly for lifers who have been in the system for some time and who may not have had the benefit previously of a coherent life sentence plan.

A good illustration of the apparent perversity of the system is provided by Casey (1996), a lifer (adopting a pseudonym) who had already served 14 years, the last two and a half years in Cat. D conditions, when it was decided on the strength of a psychologist's assessment that he should be assessed for the SOTP (see page 41) and to this end was transferred on an ostensibly temporary basis (30 days) to a closed local prison, leaving much of his property at his open prison. Having spent two years in Grendon at an earlier stage and following ten successful home leaves as well as other unsupervised experiences of temporary release, he felt that an SOTP assessment was unnecessary. On arrival at the closed prison, he learnt that this prison did not undertake the SOTP assessment. His prison earnings were reduced because of lack of employment in the prison. After two months he was moved to a Cat. B establishment where assessment was available and housed on a Vulnerable Prisoners Unit. Casey comments:

'Apart from the damage that SOTP assessment does to lifers, their relationships, their reputation in prison and their trust in those in power, the SOTP assessment is a complete farce. There are three lifers here who were assessed as not needing SOTP care treatment but these assessments were overruled by the Home Office ... lifers have no choice. We are told that it is voluntary but refusal to comply guarantees at least a two-year knockback.'

The timing of progressive transfers can be adversely affected by the waiting lists operated by many establishments, especially those holding Cat. C prisoners, which can delay agreed moves by a year or longer.

Although transfers still remain a problem, there has been some progress of late. In response to concerns raised within the prison service regarding IPP prisoners being transferred whilst undergoing a specialist assessment, such as a mental health assessment, or follow-up treatment assessment for example, prison Governors were advised not to authorise transfer until the assessment is complete unless transfer is unavoidable for security reasons (*Lifer News*, Summer 2007).

Disciplinary Transfer

Transfers may be required for reasons other than those in furtherance of the lifer's sentence, *eg* disciplinary reasons, although *LM* para. 4.10.1 makes it clear that Governors are 'expected to make every effort to manage lifers without recourse to an automatic transfer request'. When requesting a transfer on disciplinary grounds, the request must be based on proven offences rather than suspicions. Transfers cannot take place without approval in the first instance of the Lifer Unit. With regard to High Risk prisoners, transfers between High Security prisons come under the remit of High Security Prisons Operations Unit (DSHP-OU).

The Prisons Ombudsman

The extent of the Prisons Ombudsman's remit to examine complaints about the treatment of prisoners is a delicate and evolving issue and commentators (*eg* Marshall, 1996) have suggested that the watchdog has been increasingly muzzled, as instanced by recent complaints by lifers about adverse transfers or refusals to authorise favourable transfers. Marshall (1996) highlights the case of a lifer transferred by ministerial decision from a PRES (pre-release employment scheme) hostel to a Cat. C prison. Lifer Section (as it then was) refused to provide papers requested by the Ombudsman, arguing that ministers' decisions and advice to ministers were outside the Ombudsman's remit. In the case of a high profile mandatory lifer still held in a Cat. B prison after 30 years, the Ombudsman reported that the only explanation for the Home Office's decision appeared to be fear of press criticism if the lifer was seen to be treated more leniently and recommended a transfer to Cat. C conditions. The Home Office has reportedly responded with a snubbing indication that there is 'not the slightest possibility' of the Home Secretary agreeing to this request (*The Observer*, 7 July 1996).

Allocation to Grendon

Grendon received full accreditation as a Therapeutic Community in 2004. Grendon is a Cat. B prison which aims 'to provide a service to other prisons, by receiving voluntary prisoners via the Grendon application booklet. Grendon provides an environment for those who have expressed a wish to change and are motivated to be treated' (PSO 4700).

Any prospective applicant would have to fulfil the criteria set out in the application handbook as well as being free from any psychotropic medication and will need to provide two consecutive negative MDTs (Mandatory Drug Tests). Prisoners should expect to stay for at least two to three years in order to complete therapy. Grendon's own reconviction study indicates that those who stay over 18 months in therapy show a marked reduction in recidivism compared to those who leave before 18 months and even more compared with the general adult male convicted prisoner population.

Allocation to Therapeutic Communities

In addition to Grendon, therapeutic communities can be found in Dovegate, Gartree and Blundeston for adults, Aylesbury for young male offenders and at Winchester Westhill and Send for women. Although each will have specific criteria, PSO 4700 lists the following general criteria for lifer applicants:

- Must have more than 18 months to serve prior to next review.

- Must have been off Cat. A status for the last 12 months.

- Must meet 'drug-free' criteria – usually at least two months drug-free prior to transfer.

- Must have no diagnosis of mental illness.

- Must have comprehension of rules/sign compact/contract of understanding.

- Must accept responsibility for offence.

- Must meet self-harm criteria – usually at least two months free of serious self-harm prior to transfer.

Supervised Outside Activities

Some life sentence prisoners are considered appropriate for escorted absences to participate in outside activities. This is distinct from temporary release licence (detailed in Chapter 6). Escorted absence may be granted to lifers in any of the following locations:

- in Cat. D, after eight weeks;

- in Cat. C with a provisional release date, but only after at least six months;

- In Cat. C without a provisional release date but within one year of Parole Board review (*ie* the earliest a Cat. C lifer may be granted escorted absence will be four years before their tariff expiry). An application can be made after six months.

Lifers Subject to Deportation

Any foreign national who is serving a life sentence will not be released and deported until both the Parole Board and Home Secretary are of the belief that they do not pose any risk to the public. It is likely that foreign nationals serving life will experience difficulty in securing open conditions because of the fear of absconding, although each case should be considered on its own merits. Once release and deportation is approved, the lifer will be held in custody under the Immigration Act 1971 whilst arrangements are made for removal. Licence conditions cease to apply once the lifer has left the jurisdiction of the UK.

CONTACT WITH THE PROBATION SERVICE: AN OVERVIEW

The principle and intentions are clear enough. The lifer will have regular contact with the Probation Service throughout their period in prison from remand to release and whilst under supervision in the community on licence. This sustained responsibility requires a high level of communication between the designated home area offender manager and the seconded prison-based colleagues and between seconded officers and prison staff, and close co-operation with LRRS. Less is known of the realities of building and sustaining a relationship with the prisoner themselves. This section aims to summarise the limited empirical evidence.

We know rather more about lifers' experience of the Probation Service on licence than during the custodial phase of their sentence (see Coker and Martin (1985), outlined in Chapter 9). As regards contact between lifers and prison-based probation officers (PPOs), some clues can be gleaned from McFarlane's (1995) small-scale study of long-term prisoners in HMP Parkhurst in 1990–91. Interviews with 14 prisoners, including an unspecified number of lifers, all of whom had participated in a pattern of planned work with PPOs, identified various obstacles to fruitful contact, including: lack of ready access on the wings; negative views held by other prisoners that can inhibit those wanting to seek help; reluctance to use the applications system or 'shared working' arrangements if these are experienced as an off-putting filtering system; stereotypical perceptions of PPOs and the assumption that they are primarily concerned with family and marital issues and counselling; a stance that discussion of offending is a 'wind-up' (though lifers were less likely to hold this view); a resentment that PPOs' reports would be written on the basis of limited and ill-informed contact; a belief among foreign national prisoners that they do not receive equal service and the same priority as British prisoners. Where prisoners had overcome such barriers, real or assumed, or were impressed by the efforts made by PPOs to contact them, they were generally very positive about the help, friendship and challenges offered. In identifying the qualities rated by prisoners as the mark of a 'good probation officer', McFarlane notes that the descriptions 'read like an old-style casework book': positive listening, not giving direct advice but helping the prisoner to find their own solutions, understanding and acceptance, reliability, good communication, tact and respecting confidentiality, appropriate boundary setting and encouragement. 'It seemed as though these experienced consumers of the Probation Service could recognise a good service when they saw it and were willing to take advantage of it.'

Williams' interviews in 1991 with 19 long-term prisoners in a male disposal prison about their experience of 'home' probation officers produced somewhat similar findings. As a starting point it was important to acknowledge that probation officers are 'generally of peripheral importance to prisoners' lives' but, for some informants, 'there were times when throughcare assumed a major importance', even where these men had previously had little time for probation officers or held a somewhat jaundiced view of probation's worth. Overall, Williams found that long-termers sought 'some kind of personal relationship and rapport with probation officers'. That rapport could be readily enhanced if probation officers were able to demonstrate the following qualities:

Consistency and Personal Service: sustained case responsibility and staying power, despite shifts of role and change of function within the home area Service.

Honesty: giving prisoners a clear indication of what their chances are within the system; admitting one's uncertainties and lack of knowledge when faced with unfamiliar issues; being open about the level of involvement on offer.

Courtesy: keeping prisoners in touch with progress in enquiries or action on their behalf; notifying them of planned dates of visits or cancelled visits.

Reliability: delivering on promises and avoiding unrealistic undertakings.

Knowledge of the System: being well informed about the lifer system and current policy, to give prisoners accurate information and expectations.

Williams notes earlier research indications (Coker and Martin) that lifers 'without exception ... thought that the first meeting (between lifer and prospective licence supervisor) should not be arranged until after a possible release date was known', a preference clearly at odds with current expectations of sound practice based on the belief that premature contact invades privacy and generates false hopes. Most of the prisoners in his sample supported earlier contact, valuing patient, long-term work, thus allowing (for example) their officer to be able to 'see the difference ... between now and then'.

A Quality and Effectiveness Inspection Report on the work of one Probation Service (HM Inspectorate of Probation, 1996b) makes the point that the nature of the life sentence sometimes makes it 'difficult to pace the work and establish or sustain a focus for supervision, particularly during the pre-release state'. The Inspectorate notes the difficulties in risk assessment, given that at least half of the lifers with whom the Service had contact 'appeared especially dangerous because of their behaviour or attitudes before or during sentence' and 'several appeared not to appreciate the risk they continued to pose to others, or were manipulative or intimidating'.

'Supervising officers have to foster a professional relationship based on trust, openness and respect, yet remain sufficiently detached to be alert to signs that the offender might pose a risk to others.'

In a similar vein, Barter (1996) draws on experience as a prison probation officer with responsibility for lifers at a late stage of sentence in a PRES hostel to warn of dangers of complacency which can affect probation officers over lengthy periods of throughcare. Though release plans should normally be well established by this late stage of sentence, she noted the surprising number of instances where planning was still very tentative or late changes of plan proved necessary. Relationships may dissolve or be kindled unexpectedly, the Home Office may determine late in the day that the lifer should not return to their previous home area, or poor practice by the home probation officer may prompt a major re-think. A change of plan often requires a change of officer, often an unwelcome and demoralising experience for the lifer, though a new officer may facilitate a helpful re-assessment or clarification of expectations. Re-assessment may raise concerns that had previously been glossed over and this may delay or postpone the lifer's release. Barter recognises the 'awesome powers' that probation officers can wield through 'honest risk assessment', but notes the alternative dangers of naïve expectations of a lifer's capacity to cope which can cause some lifers to be released prematurely when it should have been recognised that they were not yet ready to cope with freedom. She also notes the real difficulties at times of combining clear-eyed offence-based risk assessment with the competing demands of the welter of practicalities involved in release arrangements. For a recent account of sustained probation work with a lifer before and after release, see Aust (1996).

GROUPWORK WITH LIFERS

A 1994 survey (Morrissey, 1995) of 37 prison establishments of all types, holding men and women lifers and having the benefit of psychological services, has suggested three kinds of groupwork provision for lifers: information, support and treatment. Overall, provision tends to be confined to the prisons that specialise in lifer management and it is sometimes a matter of chance whether a lifer is placed in an establishment that can address their particular needs.

Information-Based Groups

Fifteen establishments sought to meet lifers' needs for information about the life sentence system and lifer management policy, both in the early phase of sentence and in mid-sentence stage, when lifers may value help in keeping up-to-date with new policies and processes and other developments. Most lifer Main Centres provide a lifer induction group of some kind, though of varying depth and duration. The five day course at Wormwood Scrubs, allowing lifers to meet the professionals involved in their assessment and participate in 'interactive exercises' to increase trust and support, is considered a model of good practice. For lifers in mid-career who may not have received any formal initial training or need more information on progressing through the system, the need is recognised by most dispersal prisons but only by a minority of Cat. B and C prisons. Only two out of eleven Cat. B prisons and two of seven Cat. C prisons surveyed made regular provision, usually by meeting one afternoon a week.

At the pre-release stage in open conditions, only one of the Cat. D establishments surveyed reported offering an information-based course aimed specifically for lifers, *ie* Leyhill Prison's Lifers' Skills course addressing community survival needs but not the more complex area of sexual relationships, a significant omission given the number of lifers who may never have had an adult sexual relationship or otherwise be very distanced from relevant experience.

Supportive Groups

Given evidence of the high level of emotional anxiety or confusion in the early phase of sentence, groupwork at this stage can provide valuable support, alongside more structured training programmes addressing skills and strategies in coping with sentence. It was thus surprising that only two of the six main Lifer Centres, together with one of five dispersal prisons and three of 11 Cat. B establishments surveyed, made any provision of this nature. Several prisons had 'lifer discussion groups' but only a few focused specifically on feelings and anxieties. Addressing lifers' rarely met support needs in mid-sentence, Morrissey comments that there is also 'a place for more structured supportive groups that deal with the particular issue of transition from one category of prison to another', a well-known source of stress and uncertainty. None of the four open establishments provided supportive groups, despite an arguable need to address the demands of leaving the security and boundaries of imprisonment.

Groups Addressing Offending

As lifers are now required to address their offending and related behaviour before they can achieve significant progress towards release, this is probably the most crucial focus of groupwork provision. Current management policy expects that lifers should have successfully addressed areas of concern about their offending before reaching open conditions, because of the widespread belief that open prison is not an appropriate environment to begin treatment which can heighten anxiety and the risk of absconding.

Programme availability varies from establishment to establishment and not all prisons will offer the same interventions. In *Cawser v Home Secretary* (2004), the Court of Appeal found that the Secretary of State was within the limits of resources available providing a reasonable number of programmes to prisoners and that the Home Secretary was not acting irrationally by not prioritising life sentence prisoners over determinate sentence prisoners when it came to access to programmes (*Prison Law Reports*, 166).

In addition to the non-accredited programmes (such as alcohol misuse, for example), the main programmes offered are:

• Enhanced Thinking Skills (ETS).

• Controlling Anger and Learning to Manage it (CALM).

• Cognitive Skills Change Programme (CSCP).

• Sex Offender Treatment Programme (SOTP) – Core, Extended, Booster, Rolling and Adapted.

Although ETS is an accredited offending behaviour programme, it is deemed to be suitable for offenders who deny guilt of their index offence and participants will not be asked to give details of the offence unless they choose to do so (*LM* Chapter 7, para. 7.2).

Successful completion of ETS is usually a pre-requisite for entry onto SOTP and CALM. In an Home Office evaluation of the prison-run SOTP, researchers concluded (and it should be of interest to Offender Managers assessing risk to note conclusion 2) that:

1. The Core Programme has a significant impact on sexual and violent reconviction for medium-risk offenders and is also successful at reducing reconviction rates for low-risk offenders.

2. The areas targeted by the SOTP Core Programme do not seem sufficient for reducing reconviction rates on High Risk offenders. Additional treatment should be provided to High Risk Sex Offenders.

3. The Core Programmes' impact appears to have a wider effect in that although the programme focuses explicitly on sexual offenders, violent offending is also reduced by participation in the programme (Friendship, Mann & Beech, 2003).

For an account of a probation-run group for lifers who had killed their partners, see Knight, 1996).

RELEASE ON COMPASSIONATE GROUNDS

The Home Secretary has discretion to release a life sentence prisoner at any time under s30 of the Crime (Sentences) Act 1997. Before exercising this power the Home Secretary must consult the Parole Board. The Prison Governor must refer any case where release on compassionate grounds is being considered to the LRRS. The supervising offender manager will need to furnish the seconded probation staff with a report containing a proposed release plan, which will include details of the arrangements for the prisoner's care and treatment once released. *LM* Chapter 12 lists the criteria for compassionate release on medical grounds for life sentence prisoners (including IPPs) which are:

*   the prisoner is suffering from a terminal illness and death is likely to occur shortly, or the lifer is incapacitated;

*   the risk of re-offending is minimal; and

*   there are adequate arrangements for the prisoner's care and treatment outside prison; and

*   early release will bring some significant benefit to the prisoner or his/her family.

5
THE IMPACT OF LIFE IMPRISONMENT

'Prison yesterday, last week, last month, last year; prison tomorrow, next week, next month, next year. When was yesterday, what happened, I don't remember it? Due to general lack of interest tomorrow has been cancelled. Whatever point you're at, that's all you can say. Sometimes you get a wave of depression sweeps over you, other times you're just numb.'

'Alan Robinson' in Parker (1990)

'You want to know what I dream about? Just being outside at night. Just thinking, 'Right, it's two a.m., I'm taking the dog for a walk.' 'It's five a.m., pissing down with rain, but I'm going out for a run.' Because I want to. Because I can.

'Paddy' in Hulme (2000)

Assumptions can easily be made about the devastating impact of indeterminacy, as a potent and accumulating source of heightened anxieties, learnt helplessness, feelings of powerlessness and depression. Such impressions can be drawn from anecdote, such as Tony Parker's interviews with imprisoned murderers from which the quote above is taken, or from Cohen and Taylor's account (1981) of the obsessive fears of psychological deterioration experienced by long-term prisoners in Durham prison's high security wing. Empirical evidence of any adverse psychological impact or damage is far less obvious. Research findings are somewhat patchy and inconclusive, sometimes contradictory and often quite old, as well as being frequently small-scale and methodologically narrow. Our knowledge of the problems and patterns of long-term imprisonment is thus rather tentative and the following account seeks simply to summarise studies undertaken within the prison system of England and Wales and in comparable jurisdictions in the last 20 years, all of which suggest that any overly deterministic view of the impact of life imprisonment is simplistic. It will be noted how little light these studies throw on lifers' specific experiences of review procedures and the cautious pace of decision making, when it can appear that the system has overlooked them or has failed to recognise effort made or change achieved. Prisoners' autobiographical accounts provide an alternative authentic glimpse; in addition to Parker (1990), see also 'Zeno' (1968), Parker (1995), Shannon and Morgan (1996) and Hulme (2000).

Manslaughter United, Chris Hulme's book about a football team made up of lifers at HMP Kingston, reveals the complexity and frequent contradictions involved in serving a life sentence, and how lifers cope with serving a long sentence and dealing with their guilt and remorse: As 'Jonah' illustrates:

'It wasn't until about eleven years after my conviction that I started talking about my crime. One day, I spoke to this probation officer ... It was one of those situations where you felt confident. He was very relaxed in his job and in his approach. I just broke down and told him the actual story. It was the first time it had come out from A to Z. I was still using a lot of distortions about why I committed the murder. Blaming people, you know what I mean? But the floodgates opened believe me. That was my first sign of remorse, in terms of talking about the crime and breaking it down. He just let me get on with the story ... It was then continuously on my mind, you know: life means life and all this business. And I've taken someone else's life. You can't replace it. You recognise you can't replace it.'

(Hulme, 2000)

'Ray', speaking to Yvonne Jewkes, expressed mixed feelings regarding his status of a lifer on a designated 'lifer wing':

'Lifers and staff come to a nice understanding. If someone gets a pasting they wouldn't grass, but in all probability the staff would probably turn a blind eye anyway. I like being on an all-lifer wing because it's more peaceful and because the staff understand that we want to be left alone. But I suppose on balance I'd prefer a mixed wing because it stops it getting stale, you get to see fresh faces and they bring in news from the outside.'

(Jewkes, 2002)

Jewkes found hostility to lifers from other prisoners. Bill, serving five years, explains:

'Lifers always get more. In some prisons I've been in only the lifers can wear their own clothes. Here (HMP Stocken) they can go and sit out on the grass in the summer. It's like you have to kill someone to get privileges.'

RESEARCH ON LONG-TERM IMPRISONMENT
The studies summarised in this section were undertaken in England and Wales unless otherwise stated.

Measuring Psychological Change
Administering various intellectual and attitudinal tests to 200 long-term (determinate and indeterminate) male prisoners, a Durham University team (*eg* Bolton, 1976) found no evidence of psychological deterioration and few differences in the attitudes of those who had served an average of 11 years in comparison to those who were at an early stage in their sentence, though

men who had served longer showed some decline in 'self-evaluation'. Verbal intelligence showed a significant increase over time.

Focus of Concerns

Interviewing 56 male lifers at Wakefield prison at different stages of sentence, Lawton (1977) found that men who had served longer were more likely to express concern about broad issues of personal autonomy, dignity and communication with authority, while newly received men, especially those with little or no previous experience of prison, were more likely to be concerned with day-to-day details of their immediate environment.

Whittington (1994), a prison education co-ordinator at HMP Gartree, asked 102 lifers who had served various lengths of sentence from under three years to over 20 years to list the concerns that they felt would most occupy lifers at various stages within the first nine years of sentence. Though the research report is somewhat slight and confusing, the following returns appear noteworthy:

(i) *Concerns about self-image and psychological survival*
The fear of institutionalisation was very real. The lifers surveyed all mentioned worries whether they could 'do the time' and complete sentence without loss of identity, individuality and self-esteem. Such concerns appeared strongest between the end of the first year and year six. That said, most indicated that they were coping well enough with their sentence, despite feelings of loneliness and aimlessness.

(ii) *Concerns about the future*
Asked how to describe their general outlook since conviction, the lifers most frequently identified worries about the future, followed by loneliness and lack of purpose. Though these concerns are reported as dominant between years six and nine, 'negative feelings' broadly decreased over the first seven years of imprisonment but, thereafter, the feelings of those with no previous experience of prison became more negative, while those with previous prison experience continued to become more positive.

(iii) *Concerns with their crime*
This was identified by only a small percentage of prisoners and, even in this limited respect, was a feature only of the first three years of sentence, particularly the year following conviction.

Stress

Richards (1978) asked two groups of male long-term prisoners (mostly lifers), those in the first 18 months of sentence and those who had served more than eight years, located in 'an easy nick', to rate a list of 20 stresses associated with imprisonment for their frequency and intensity of occurrence. The two groups responded in a very similar way. The five most severe problems were: missing somebody, feeling that your life is being wasted, feeling sexually frustrated, missing little 'luxuries', missing social life. The five least severe problems were: losing self-confidence, feeling angry with the world, being afraid of dying before release, being afraid of going mad, feeling suicidal. On the whole the men did not see their imprisonment as a fundamental threat to their mental health. Those problems rated as most severe related to the deprivation of relationships in and with the outside rather than to the privations of prison life.

Richards' British study was replicated by Flanagan (1980), with 59 long-term prisoners, 60% of whom were lifers, who had served at least five years continuous confinement in maximum security prisons in the United States, with very similar results. Addressing the prevailing hardship of separation from family and friends which, in the words of one respondent, 'gets harder as the years pass' and the fear of irrevocable loss of such relationships, Flanagan notes:

'Some long-term inmates cauterise these relationships as a means of avoiding the anxiety and despair that accompany the separation. For the majority of prisoners who do not attempt this strategy, family ties become a two-edged sword over the years, providing encouragement and support and at the same time making it more difficult to do time.'

Evolution of Attitude

Sapsford (1978, 1983) studied three matched groups of homicide lifers in a maximum security prison, comparing 20 newly-sentenced men with 20 in their sixth year and ten 'hardcore' men who had passed the average date for release (at that time, 11 years). At the start of the sentence, the shock was evidently very great: 'suddenly they have lost the whole pattern of their lives and the whole of the reinforcement to which they are accustomed'. Three-quarters of the total sample received medical reports at reception which suggested some degree of psychological disturbance. Some 30% showed considerable anxiety, being either 'timid and withdrawn' or manifesting a high degree of 'emotionality and intropunitive hostility', *ie* being belligerent, tense and prone to temper outbursts.

'With only four exceptions – men who were sustained by outside contacts or already familiar with institutions or deprived lifestyles, or not yet considering the sentence as inevitable – all of the lifers in the sample showed considerable emotional disturbance during the year or so following their reception into prison.'

Those who had spent more time on sentence showed four traits, over and above the effects of ageing:

(i) reduction in their 'future time' perspective (*ie* the future events they mentioned in interview were not so distant from the present);

(ii) greater tendency to talk and think about the past;

(iii) increased introversion/less interest in social activities and 'out-going' behaviour;

(iv) more dependence on routine, even in petty matters, and less ability to take even trivial decisions for oneself.

Longer serving men showed no indication of reduced interest in the outside world or the possibility of release, nor of increased apathy, but the two long-serving groups had less actual involvement with outsiders, having nearly all lost contact with their pre-sentence partners. Hardcore men showed a greater tendency to see themselves as aligned with staff but this was not reflected in the staff's view of them.

Adaptation and Coping

Sapsford (1983) cautioned that changes over time should not be interpreted as involuntary processes of deterioration or as a reflection of 'learned helplessness', but as adaptations and coping strategies in face of the psychological strains of prolonged detention. King and Elliott (1977) offer one of the best known attempts to provide a typology of prisoner survival strategies, based on their study of HMP Albany, then a dispersal prison:

(i) *uncertain negative retreat*: difficulties in coping both with staff and other prisoners;

(ii) *secondary comfort indulgence*: making the best of available comforts;

(iii) *jailing*: considerable involvement in the prisoner social system, including consumption and trading of contraband;

(iv) *gleaning*: frequent contact with specialist staff and resources such as education courses or groupwork programmes, acquiring qualifications etc;

(v) *opportunism*: selective exploitation of both the prisoner social system and specialist staff resources;

(vi) *'doing your bird'*: keeping out of trouble and avoiding the attentions of staff and other prisoners but retaining the respect of both.

Based on Canadian research, Porporino and Zamble (1984) concluded that poor coping skills in prison reflect maladaptive functioning in the community prior to imprisonment.

Prisoners coping badly inside were more likely to have been unemployed and without secure emotional partnerships outside. They suggested that imprisonment can reinforce maladaptive ways of coping.

Experience of Isolation

Based on their work as probation officers with male lifers at Nottingham prison, Raban *et al* (1983) suggested three forms of isolation commonly experienced:

(i) *physical isolation*: long periods without visits, feeling alienated from family, no 'fellowship' with 'ordinary' people; being cut off from 'every good thing in the world';

(ii) *powerlessness*: limited scope to take decisions for self, feeling of being kept in the dark about plans for the future, frequently resulting in a lack of reality and sense of what is important;

(iii) *emotional*: many lifers described resort to a self-imposed isolation as a survival tactic in the early years of their sentence. Sometimes the sense of isolation became so acute that prisoners felt unable to initiate communication themselves, so that they became increasingly overlooked.

'The totality of sentence led several lifers to feel at times that they were beyond help and so were presumably difficult to reach by prison and probation staff.'

Some experienced this most acutely in the first 18 months and several during the second to fifth years, but 60% felt that it applied for most of the time.

Developing a Long-Term Perspective

Based on interviews with 59 long-term prisoners in maximum security prisons in a USA North-Eastern state, 60% of whom were serving life, who had served at least five years, Flanagan (1981) identified a common pattern of thinking among long-term prisoners:

(i) *Avoidance of conflict/trouble*: mind your own business, adjust to authority, stay alert to the cues of the prison environment, choose your associates wisely;

(ii) *Use time constructively*: value constructive opportunities and goals in education and skill development, immerse yourself in 'projects' (ranging from craft activities to 'legal' work on your own case);

(iii) *Handle problems for yourself*: don't take your fears and problems to others to solve, demonstrate your ability to 'do time' successfully;

(iv) *Distinguish yourself from short-termers* who are seen as 'different', more impulsive, reckless, etc.

Flanagan thus considers that long-term prisoners adhere to the norms of their sub-culture, with expectations of 'coping', self-reliance and 'doing your time'.

He suggests that this can cause an under-response to questions which aim to identify emotional difficulties.

'Many inmates do not perceive anyone to whom they can turn for help. Fellow inmates either cannot be trusted or have problems of their own; family members are not seen as alternatives ('it would be unfair to unburden oneself'/'I've already hurt them enough'/'the least I can do is try to reassure them that everything is going OK'); institutional staff are viewed as unconcerned. Given these constraints, it is not surprising that these subjects report that most problems are handled by 'keeping it to myself'.'

Zamble (1992) studied 25 long-term prisoners in Ontario, 21 of whom being lifers, who had served a mean time of 7.1 years. After considerable initial psychological discomfort, his sample had experienced a slow, gradual amelioration and there was no evidence for any general or widespread deteriorative effects of prolonged incarceration. Instead, the general pattern was of improved emotional state, health and conduct within prison over time. Despite some instances of maladaptive behaviour patterns, the prisoners gained in their adaptive abilities and learnt to avoid becoming embroiled in conflict or disruptive behaviour which could interfere with their prospects of release. Though there was no evidence of social isolation, many prisoners largely withdrew from the diffuse social networks typical of prisoner interaction. Instead, they spent much of their discretionary time in their cells and, when they did socialise, it was primarily with one or two close friends. Socialisation thus centred on a small number of trusted 'inside' friends or relationships with people outside. Prisoners planned their activities around longer-term gains with a focus on their future life after release. They seemed to be living within their own personal niches and routines, inside the prison but separate and apart from its ordinary discourse. Their cognitive focus was elsewhere. They began to define themselves differently, as 'persons living in prison, not offenders doing time'.

Powerlessness and Mistrust

Mitchell (1990) interviewed 82 lifers in the latter stage of their sentence, all except one being either in open prison or in a PRES hostel. More than three-quarters maintained that imprisonment had had no apparent adverse effect on them. However, they expressed an 'overwhelming lack of trust and confidence in the efficiency and reliability of the penal system' and 'only rarely did any of them feel able to have confidence in prison staff'. 'These points were symptomatic of a general feeling of helplessness and isolation ... lifers tended not to feel sufficiently secure in the belief that making the appropriate effort would be to their advantage.'

Survival Skills

Based on a study of 239 released lifers who had served an average of nine years, Coker and Martin (1985) concluded that they had not been seriously damaged or incapacitated by their experiences. Though their contact with the outside world might atrophy through neglect, coping with their sentences had required considerable personal resources and the sample showed 'a fierce desire for independence and a capacity to manage their lives competently'.

For a detailed study of the emotional and sexual adaptations by men as a result of long-term imprisonment, see Hornby (2007).

Women Lifers

Genders and Player (1988) provide a rare assessment of the particular predicament of women serving life, based on a short study of H Wing at HMP Durham, the main centre for women in the first phase of sentence. It then held 25 lifers and 11 long determinate sentenced women. The environment of this small unit located within a male prison appeared claustrophobic and restricted, offering very limited resources and little privacy. For those who had killed to escape oppressive or violent relationships with men, the proximity and attentions of male prisoners were experienced as intrusive, threatening or demeaning.

As women facing indefinite detention, the Durham lifers were acutely conscious either of the potential loss of parental rights in respect of their children or of the lost prospect of having children. Unable to provide support to their families, fearing loss of their sexual attraction and doubtful of their capacity to relate to men on release after their particular experience and with such an exceptional identity, women reported that they felt stripped of their sense of womanhood. Women commonly expressed their sense of being stalled by the artificial environment in their capacity to express emotion and to act naturally. They felt that they would be assessed adversely no matter how they behaved. Unsurprisingly, staff felt women were unduly preoccupied with day-to-day minor details or with their health problems. Prisoners were able to recognise their tendency to obsessions, compulsive behaviour and forgetfulness. They feared the deterioration of their health and worried about the high number of hysterectomies undergone by long sentence women.

While their study may be somewhat dated and perhaps under-rates women's capacity for survival, Genders and Player suggest the importance of creating a custodial milieu in which women can safely explore their emotions, concerns and anxieties, enhance their communication skills, receive therapeutic help and reduce their sense of exposure and vulnerability. The Prison Service's assumption that women can be dealt with by a scaled-down version of the male lifer system appears to ignore crucial structural and psychological differences.

Yvonne Jewkes (2005) outlines the impact of a disrupted lifecourse for life-sentenced female prisoners. The lifecourse embodies significant events and rites of passage through every person's life, such as entry into the workforce, marriage, raising a family and retirement. In Western cultures, women live their lives against a background of assumptions that they want to be or will be mothers. However, for a woman serving a life sentence, the event of having children is lost. Drawing on studies of infertility, Jewkes argues that women who are unable to have children frequently grieve for their loss and so:

'It is likely that women in prison who are childless and who have had the opportunity to be mothers denied them because of the sentence they are serving, may experience a similar sense of loss and grief for the child they never had.'

(Jewkes, 2005)

Much has been written about the impact of the prison sentence, including life sentences, on families and children. For a detailed literature review and the current policy response, see Rijnenberg (2007).

In a study of long-term women prisoners in a Louisiana prison, MacKenzie *et al* (1989) found no significant differences in the levels of anxiety or psychological state between newly sentenced women and those who had served a substantial period of sentence. Those recently sentenced felt less in control of events, more concerned with issues of personal safety and more likely to resort to 'play family' participation, in which prisoners adopted caring, dependent or partnered quasi-family roles towards each other, as a mutual method of coping.

Serving the Life Sentence in Old Age

According to Elaine Crawley (2005), the number of prisoners over state retirement age, particularly among men, is increasing. Within this older population are more life sentence prisoners, in whom Crawley found little hope for the future and a fatalistic outlook on death due to infirmity and old age in prison:

'Sadly, but perhaps unsurprisingly, a few of our interviewees – all of them 'natural lifers' with no expectation of release – were also deeply distressed. Our conversations with these men were often punctuated, much to our own distress, by suppressed sobs, streams of tears and cries of bitterness and exasperation. As one man commented, his prison sentence had marked 'the end of everything.' He knew that for him, release – the light at the end of the tunnel that most prisoners do eventually get to see – would never come. Although the thought of death in confinement is, for most prisoners, appalling; for prisoners like this man, it represents release:

61

'Every night I hope I don't see the morning because there is no life for me. I am depressed twenty-four hours a day, and I know I'm going to die in prison. I hope I don't wake up – there is no life for me.'

All the natural lifers voiced a deep yearning to die as free men and in the company of a loving family and friends. Since this was not possible, however, a prison death could not come too soon.'

PSYCHIATRIC DISORDER

According to somewhat dated Home Office research (based on 452 men sentenced to life for murder or diminished responsibility manslaughter between 1956 and 1965), 43% had been diagnosed as mentally disordered by the date of their conviction, 11% having been considered sufficiently disordered at some stage prior to their crime to have been admitted to a psychiatric hospital. Some 22% of diminished responsibility cases and 5% of the murderers in the sample were transferred to hospital at some stage of sentence, mostly within the first two years (Sapsford and Banks, 1979).

As part of a larger study of psychiatric disorder in the sentenced male prison population in 1988–89 (Gunn *et al*, 1991), Swinton *et al* (1994) assessed a sample of 170 lifers (87% being mandatory), by studying their prison files and conducting a psychiatric interview. The sample contained significantly more subjects who were in the early part of their sentence (less than five years served) than the lifer population as a whole, and so cannot be considered to be entirely representative. Various psychiatric diagnoses (including alcohol dependence) were made in 69 (41%) cases. Of six assessed as psychotic (schizophrenia or paranoia) and 38 considered personality disordered or sexually disordered, 13 cases (8%) of the sample, five psychotic and eight disordered, were rated as needing hospital admission and 48 (28%) as requiring psychiatric treatment of some kind. Appropriate treatment was being provided within prison in 12 of these cases. The incidence of mental disorder was not associated with length of stay in prison.

Though there must be caution in extrapolating these findings, the figures suggest that 3.5% of the male lifer population have psychotic disorders and 7.7% may need hospital admission. Though lifers in this sample were found to have a substantially higher prevalence of personality disorder than other male prisoners, this finding could be because life prisoners' behaviour problems are much better documented in case files. The prevalence of psychoses in the sample was significantly lower than Taylor's (1986) finding that 10% of 183 lifers known to the Inner London Probation Service were suffering schizophrenia, but the London sample included all known lifers whether in custody, transferred to hospital or on licence, whereas the Swinton sample excluded any subject to hospital transfer under MHA 1983 s47. Swinton points out that the five psychotic lifers assessed as suitable for hospital admission were well known to prison medical staff but remained in prison because they did not pose a serious management problem and psychiatric hospitals are reluctant to take such individuals, partly because the Home Office would require them to be placed on wards with a high level of security, even if this was not necessary on clinical grounds.

The status and procedures governing lifers transferred to psychiatric hospital are addressed in Chapter 11.

SELF-INFLICTED DEATHS

There is considerable evidence of a link between homicidal crime and self-harm. Approximately 5% of remanded homicide suspects die while awaiting trial, almost all by suicide. Dooley (1990) found that prisoners convicted of murder accounted for 15.6% of all sentenced prisoner suicides in the period 1972–1987, though they represented only 3.6% of the sentenced population. In the study of lifers by Swinton *et al* (1994, see page 62) nearly a quarter of the sample had a history of self-harm and 'one in six had probably attempted suicide (substantially more than reported by other sentenced prisoners)'.

In the five-year period between 1990–1994, 30 self-inflicted deaths of post-sentence lifers were recorded, compared with 210 non-lifers (including remand prisoners who might be anticipating a life sentence). Restated more meaningfully as rates per 10,000 of the two populations, the figures show that the incidence of self-inflicted death in the lifer population in any year is generally higher than in the non-lifer population. Over the five years, the rate of self-inflicted death among lifers was twice as high as in the non-lifer population (*Lifer News*, Autumn 1995).

Between 1996 and 1999, 21% of all self-inflicted deaths in prisons were among lifers; a group that constituted just 9% of the prison population in 1999 (Sattar, 2001). More recent figures tell an increasingly sombre story. In 2004/05 there were 135.9 self-inflicted deaths per 100,000 of the average prison population. That translates into 95 prisoners; of whom 83 died by hanging themselves, 10 died from a ligature and 2 from cuts to throats or wrists. 13 of those 95 prisoners were women (Coyle, 2005).

In a longer-scale survey, Truscott (1995) studied the records of male lifers (including men remanded on murder charges) who committed suicide in the period 1980–1993, to gain a better understanding of which lifers may be most at risk of self-inflicted death. One-third of those studied had died while on remand, the majority after two months of custody. Most deaths occurred at night and eight out of ten died by hanging. Two broad groups of prisoners emerged from the study as high risk categories: men with a higher number of previous convictions and, in particular, convictions for violence, who now turned their capacity for violence upon themselves; distressed men who felt very badly about themselves, and appeared desperately lonely and with little to live for and were probably very troubled by guilt, particularly where they had killed their partner. There is as yet little evidence to show at what stage of sentence convicted lifers are most at risk.

6
RELEASE ON TEMPORARY LICENCE

RELEASE ON TEMPORARY LICENCE (ROTL)

Prison Rule 9 makes provision for the release of prisoners on temporary licence. Information relating to Release on Temporary Licence (ROTL) can be found in PSO 6300 which also incorporates the provisions of the CJA 2003. ROTL is a privilege, not a right, and may be revoked at any time if there is a risk to public safety issues. Where life sentence prisoners fail to return from ROTL, they are guilty of a criminal offence under s1 of the Prisoners (Return to Custody) Act 1995. An LSP4D should be completed and LRRS notified. All prison establishments should have a protocol governing local implementation and also a leaflet for prisoners containing information on ROTL.

There are now four kinds of temporary licence:

1. **Resettlement Day Release**

   Can be considered for the following reasons:

   - Reparative community work/unpaid employment;

   - Life and work skills training/education;

   - Housing;

   - Probation interviews;

   - Maintaining family ties;

   - Job-hunting activites such as attending interviews or job searching;

   - Paid employment (Resettlement Estate only);

   - Driving lessons (Resettlement Estate only);

   - Opening bank accounts.

2. **Resettlement Overnight Release**

   Resettlement overnight release (ROR) allows prisoners to spend time at their intended release address, Probation Approved Premises or hostel address, helping to establish links with family and re-integrate back into the local community. These temporary absences can also be used to facilitate interviews for work, training or accommodation. Release may also be granted for placements with Community Service Volunteers (CSV) or the Prince's Trust for younger offenders. Establishments are required to draw up a memorandum of understanding relating to the placement of prisoners with outside agencies such as CSV.

3. Childcare Resettlement Leave

Can be taken where it is established that prisoners have sole caring responsibility for a child. The onus is on the prisoner to satisfy the prison governor that they meet the definition of a sole carer early on in their sentence. In addition to this, clearly, the interests and safety of the child have to be taken into account before granting childcare resettlement leave.

4. Special Purpose Licence

Short duration temporary release, often granted at short notice. This allows prisoners who are eligible to respond to exceptional personal circumstances and to wider criminal justice needs.

Acceptable grounds for special purpose licence:

- visits to dying relatives, funerals or other tragic personal circumstances;

- prisoners who, on reception, have established general parental responsibility for a child under 16, to deal with emergencies relating to their parental duties;

- prisoners who, on release, will have sole caring responsibility of an elderly or severely disabled relative, to deal with emergencies relating to their duties;

- to attend medical out-patient appointments or in-patient requirements;

- marriage of the prisoner – usually for the period of the ceremony and no longer;

- to attend court, tribunal or inquiry proceedings (this is different to productions under the Crime (Sentences) Act 1997;

- conferences with legal advisers in exceptional circumstances;

- helping the police with their enquiries.

Eligibility for ROTL

Category A prisoners are not eligible for any type of ROTL. Life sentence prisoners will usually only be released if they are in open or semi-open conditions. Lifers cannot be released from closed conditions (except in exceptional circumstances where they have been assessed as suitable for open conditions, but cannot be transferred for medical reasons).

APPLICATIONS FOR RELEASE ON TEMPORARY LICENCE

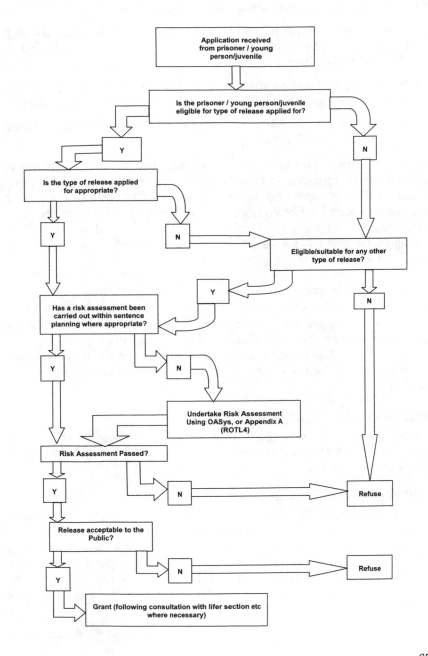

FACILITY LICENCE

A facility licence may be permitted in three circumstances:

(i) to enable participation in *'regime-related activities'* (education, training, employment, community service projects, etc.) or activities having an element of *reparation*;

(ii) *'official purposes'* such as attendance at civil court proceedings, acting as police witnesses and to visit legal advisers in exceptional circumstances;

(iii) *day visits to local towns* (lifers only), in preparation for further unsupervised activity and resettlement licences.

'Regime activities' must have a 'clear and substantive' purpose, aimed at rehabilitation or reparation, and must not have a social or recreational content. Licence will not be appropriate for any purpose which could be accomplished more appropriately later in sentence, or by release on resettlement licence or after release. Considerations of 'public acceptability' as well as public safety will apply. Licence will not be granted if release would attract 'reasonable public concern'.

Duration and Frequency

Facility licences will normally be granted on the basis of day release only and initially for one day per week. This can be increased to three days outside the prison for community projects, educational courses or work experience, at the Governor's discretion according to the prisoner's progress and performance. Periods in excess of three days per week require further Headquarters approval.

Transfers to Open Conditions

Though determinate term prisoners are normally considered suitable for unescorted transfer to or between open conditions under facility licence, lifers are explicitly excluded.

SUPERVISING OFFICER

'The potential sensitivities associated with the ROTL of life sentence prisoners make it particularly important that the risk assessment identifies the nature and extent of checks required for a life sentence prisoner during each ROTL. It is important, where possible, that the supervising probation officer (or Offender Manager) is available throughout the period of leave. This is particularly relevant to home leave as opposed to unpaid/paid work placements.'

(PSO 6300, para. 4.3.5)

Clearly, allowing lifers leave at weekends where no probation support is available is unwise, particularly for the first few grants of leave. Where the Offender Manager is on leave or away from the office, a replacement contact from within the Offender Management cluster or 'pod' needs to be identified. It is also important when considering the timing of ROTL that OMs make the prison aware of any significant anniversaries or venues, with particular reference to victims.' The Probation Service must be consulted to ensure that any victim's issues are appropriately addressed by Victim Liaison Officers (para. 4.3).

RISK ASSESSMENT
Assessment Considerations
A full OASys must be completed when ROTL is contemplated.

The main considerations to be borne in mind when considering applications are:

(i)   the risk that the prisoner would present to public safety;

(ii) the risk of further offending when released on temporary licence;

(iii) the likelihood of failure to comply with any licence conditions;

(iv) propensity to abscond;

(v)   availability of suitable accommodation if an overnight stay is contemplated;

(vi) whether the reasons for granting licence are likely to be acceptable to reasonable public opinion.

Risk Factors
The level of risk must be assessed by taking into account, as a minimum, the following factors:

(i)   offence analysis and criminal history;

(ii) (where relevant) home circumstances, including financial pressures and other family problems liable to arise over the licence period and the extent to which the prisoner and their family are realistic about being able to deal with demands of this nature. Do the prisoner's family want the prisoner to return home and will the family need any counselling? Are there particular events or dates which need to be avoided, *eg* the anniversary of an offence, or which should be included, *eg* a family celebration?

(iii) the position of known victim(s) and, where relevant, the local community;

69

(iv) previous releases on temporary licence (or the equivalent prior to the introduction of the present system);

(v) behaviour in prison, including indications of: past use or abuse of trust; violent temper or loss of control; tackling offending in a positive and successful way; denial of a sex offence ('normally an indication of an unquantifiable risk') or a non-sexual offence ('this will normally make it more difficult to assess risk although past events may give useful indications'); likelihood of bringing back contraband;

(vi) specific areas of concern, *ie* any factors in the prisoner's history that might increase risk, *eg* drug or alcohol abuse, mental disorder or stress-related illness, and the extent to which the prisoner succeeded in addressing such issues.

Consideration by the Board

Board Composition

Where a Lifer ROTL Board considers the prisoner's application, the Board should include as a minimum: a governor grade, a prison officer who knows the prisoner well (*eg* their personal officer), a seconded probation officer who knows the prisoner, psychologist, the lifer liaison officer. The Board may invite the prisoner to attend for all or part of its consideration.

Information Available to the Board

The Board should have before it:

1. the prisoner's full criminal history;

2. an up-to-date sentence plan;

3. the views of Social Services, if the individual is a risk to children;

4. a Wing report;

5. a Medical Officer's report (where appropriate);

6. a written report from the seconded probation officer (compiled in collaboration with the home area offender manager where appropriate), including:

   (a) a description of the prisoner's current offence;

   (b) the relationship, if any, to the prisoner of known victims and available information about the victim's circumstances; details of any contact by the victim with the Victim Helpline;

   (c) information about any previous convictions, in particular those involving the victim(s) of the current offence, where a connection with the prisoner remains;

(d) a description of the prisoner's home circumstances, including where appropriate:

(i) the address for the release (including the prisoner's status while there, *eg* homeowner, tenant, etc.) and whether visited;

(ii) the attitudes and situation of those who would receive the prisoner;

(iii) any indicators of the risk within the family (*eg* relationship breakdown, alcohol abuse, child abuse);

(iv) any other information relevant to the current release request;

(v) child protection issues and contact with Social Services.

The Board's Recommendations
The Board should make a written recommendation to the Governor (or to the Lifer Unit, where appropriate), including: a recommendation about the advisability of additional licence conditions; details of the dates (and address for accommodation, where appropriate) agreed with any agency undertaking supervision, where appropriate, during the leave; any other precautionary measures necessary within the establishment or to be taken by the probation service locally. The Governor should ensure that a written record is maintained showing the relevant factors taken into account when reaching a final decision and the weight given to each particular factor.

Information from the Probation Service

Requests of this nature will arise primarily where a prisoner seeks a resettlement licence. When ROTL involves the prisoner returning to the home area/address for release, the supervising officer must be asked to make enquiries about the specific proposals. In the case of resettlement overnight release, the supervising Offender Manager is required to submit a home circumstances report on Form ROTL 3, which must be sent out by the prison at least four weeks before it is required. The supervising Offender Manager should include any up-to-date information regarding Victim Liaison Officer enquiries and where it is felt additional licence conditions need to be considered.

Distant Destinations

Prisoners may not be granted release on temporary licence to any place outside the United Kingdom, Channel Islands and the Isle of Man. When a prisoner is granted a licence to a distant destination in England and Wales, the Governor may impose a condition of licence that they lodge overnight at a convenient prison locally, if one exists. This would not normally be considered unless the prisoner has been granted *compassionate* release and no alternative lodging is considered suitable.

71

Refusal of Application

Prisoners should be given written reasons for any decision to refuse their application. These should be signed by the Governor making the decision and copies of these reasons should be forwarded to the Parole and Lifer Unit at HQ. Confidential police intelligence should not be disclosed to a prisoner and careful consideration should be given before any information pertaining to victims is disclosed to a prisoner.

Additional Licence Conditions

The extra precaution of additional requirements in the lifer's temporary licence should be considered in all instances. Additional conditions should be specific, reasonable and clearly understood by the prisoner. They should be constructed to address the following critical factors, where appropriate:

(i) the need to return on time;

(ii) particular risks connected with the individual prisoner (*eg* alcohol or gambling problems);

(iii) the concerns of actual or potential victims (*eg* as to the prisoner's movements during their leave);

(iv) previous evidence of the prisoner's unreliability (*eg* failing to keep appointments or to return promptly).

DRUG TESTING

The prisoner may be subject to a drug test (under the mandatory drug testing programme, when in place at the establishment) prior to their release on temporary licence, though testing 'should be carried out on a scale in proportion to the drug problems within the prison'. Should a test prove positive, the prisoner's release on licence will normally be cancelled, 'unless there are extremely compelling circumstances in favour of it being allowed to proceed', and should give rise to disciplinary proceedings. The positive test result will also be given weight in any future risk assessment of the prisoner. Any positive voluntary drug test (VDTs) must be taken into consideration when deciding suitability for ROTL.

ROLE OF PROBATION SERVICE DURING LICENCE AND CONDITIONS OF CONTACT

In addition to the provision regarding the availability of the supervising probation officer during periods of resettlement licence, *HOC 25/95*, paragraphs 37–41 specify:

'37. In exceptional circumstances, the prison may request the Probation Service to establish contact with the offender during the period of release on temporary licence. Any such requests, together with the reasons for it, should be included in the letter accompanying ROTL 3 when it is sent to the Probation Service.

38. If the Probation Service requests a condition of contact as part of the normal throughcare process, this should be included on ROTL 3. The Service may also request that other conditions be built in, for example that the victim should not be contacted.

39. If, to the Probation Service's knowledge, the offender fails to comply with the terms of the licence or appears to present an immediate risk of harm to him/herself or the public, the Service should inform the prison duty Governor by telephone immediately.

40. The Probation Service will contact the release address after overnight release has occurred for the first time. The purpose of this contact, which may be by telephone, is to check whether the release passed satisfactorily. The Probation Service will then notify the prison accordingly.

41. If the release does proceed satisfactorily and further releases are proposed at the same address, the Probation Service will not be expected to visit the release address beforehand; contact by telephone will normally be sufficient.'

BREACH OF TEMPORARY LICENCE

PS0 6300 emphasises that breaches should be dealt with firmly and consistently and that Governors should exercise a system of random spot checks, either by telephone or by visit, to ensure that prisoners do not abuse their licence privilege, for example by meeting friends in a pub while supposed to be attending a course or visiting a hostel.

Failure to Return on Time

Late-returning prisoners can expect disciplinary proceedings against them, 'unless it is clear that such a charge is not justified' (para. 8.3). The police will be notified of a prisoner's continuing failure to return and the supervising probation officer should also be informed, normally via the prison probation department. The incident should be reported to LRRS.

Additionally, under the Prisoners (Return to Custody) Act 1995 s1, a prisoner who, without reasonable excuse, remains unlawfully at large after the expiry of their temporary release commits a summary offence punishable by six months imprisonment and/or a level 5 fine (£5,000). Similarly, an offence of this nature arises where the prisoner knows or believes that a recall order has been issued and fails, without reasonable excuse, 'to take all necessary steps for complying as soon as reasonably practicable with that order'. An offence under this provision 'shall be taken to be committed at the place where the offender was required to be detained immediately before being temporarily released'.

Criminal Offences

Any notification that a prisoner has been arrested on suspicion of a criminal offence must be reported to the Incident Reporting System (IRS), making it clear that the prisoner is believed to have committed a criminal offence (para. 7.2). Paragraph 7.2.4 specifies:

> 'If a prisoner is convicted of an offence, committed while on previous temporary release, or while UAL (Unlawfully at Large) following the expiry of a previous temporary licence, the expectation is that they will usually be unsuitable for further periods of temporary release. However, should a prisoner apply for further temporary release, the risk assessment must take account of the previous circumstances. Governors must be satisfied that the risk has been fully addressed before any further temporary release is granted.'

In a Parliamentary answer (House of Lords, 4 December 1995), Baroness Blatch indicated that a lifer convicted of an offence committed while on resettlement licence 'would be unlikely ever to receive home leave again'.

Non-Criminal Misconduct

Breach of licence conditions not involving criminal misconduct should be dealt with as a prison disciplinary offence. Prosecution for an alleged or substantiated criminal offence while on licence does not debar disciplinary action for any other breach of licence.

RECALL FROM LICENCE

A prisoner may be recalled at any time from release on temporary licence. If a prisoner is arrested but not held in custody, or misbehaves in some other way, the Governor should consider recalling them immediately. Paragraphs 7.1.2 and 7.1.3 specify:

> '7.1.2 The Governor must document all decisions to recall a prisoner from temporary licence for any reason other than a breach of licence or committing a criminal offence.'

> 7.1.3 Once a decision is made to recall a prisoner, the Governor must ask the police to take the prisoner into custody and hold him or her at the police station. The police must be asked to notify the escort contractor serving their area. The prisoner will be returned to the nearest appropriate prison or YOI.'

It is true to say that the one-time bewildering number of forms used for ROTL has now been trimmed to the relevant nine documents which are listed below.

ROTL 1: Application for Release on Temporary Licence (filled in by prisoner)

ROTL 2: Invitation for Police to Comment on Proposed ROTL (completed by police)

ROTL 3: Invitation to Probation Service to Comment on Proposed ROTL (completed by Offender Manager)

ROTL 4: Risk Assessment for ROTL (completed by prison staff using OASys)

ROTL 5: Notification of Decision on Application for ROTL (given to prisoner)

ROTL 6: Notification to Police and Probation of ROTL (sent out by prison to police and probation)

ROTL 7: Licences (accompanies prisoner and must be signed by Governor grade and prisoner)

ROTL 8: Inability to Return to Prison due to Medical Reasons (signed by prisoner and doctor)

ROTL 9: Invitation for IND to Comment/Provide Authorisation on Proposed ROTL (for use when there is a perceived immigration risk)

7
REVIEWING THE LIFE SENTENCE

All prisoners serving a life sentence are entitled to a Parole Board review shortly before the expiry of the minimum term of imprisonment. The CJA 2003 brought in new rules for those offenders convicted of murder which are explained below.

SETTING THE MINIMUM TERM FOR MURDER
All life tariffs are now set by the Judge in open court. The CJA 2003 makes allowances for the fact that, in cases of exceptional gravity, the Judge should indicate that no minimum term could properly be set. The starting points for the minimum term – or tariff as it is frequently referred to – for mandatory sentences of life imprisonment, detention during Her Majesty's pleasure and custody for life, can be located in s269 of, and Sch 21 to, the CJA 2003. A minimum term is the period of the sentence which must be served in full before early release can be ordered. So, a person convicted of murder and sentenced to 30 years would have a minimum term of 15 years, assuming that early release will be at the halfway point.

The starting point of 30 years as a minimum term would include:

- murder of a police officer or prison officer in the course of duty;

- murder involving a firearm or an explosive;

- murder carried out for gain (as in the course of a burglary for example);

- murder involving sexual or sadistic conduct;

- murder of two or more people;

- a racially or religiously aggravated murder, or one aggravated by sexual orientation.

Those offenders who were convicted of murder prior to the new provisions contained within the CJA 2003 (which came into force in January 2004) had their tariff set by the Home Secretary and can now apply for the tariff to be reset by a High Court Judge. For example, Richard Davies was convicted of murder at Swansea Crown Court in February 2002. In February 2007, his tariff was reviewed by Mr Justice Roderick Evans at the Royal Courts of Justice in London. The Judge set the tariff of 15 years and taking into account remand time this means Richard Davies can apply for parole in 2016 (*South Wales Evening Post*, 6 February 2007). In the case of Andrew Cole, who was convicted of the murder of Fiona Ovis in May 1998, the Home Secretary imposed a tariff of 15 years. On reviewing the tariff in 2006 Mr Justice Mackay reduced the minimum term to 11 years which with remand time taken into account means that Cole is eligible for parole in June 2007 (*Brecon & Radnor Express*, 28 December 2006). David Copeland was given a life sentence with a tariff set at 30 years in June 2000 for the murder of three people in a pub bombing in London. Reviewing the tariff in the High Court, Mr Justice Burton said the starting point was inevitably 'whole life' and describing the offence as 'a really exceptional case of deliberate multiple murder' and, citing grounds of 'exceptional gravity', increased the tariff to 50 years – with a deduction of 13 months and 26 days for time spent on remand (*East London Advertiser*, 2 March 2007).

SETTING THE MINIMUM TERM FOR CONSPIRACY TO MURDER

In June 2006, Colin Gunn, John Russell and Michael McNee were all convicted of conspiracy to murder Joan and John Stirland and sentenced to life imprisonment, which is the maximum sentence that can be awarded in cases of conspiracy to murder. Because the murders were committed after 18 December 2003 the court, when imposing a mandatory life sentence, would be obliged when fixing the minimum term to have regard to the principles set out in Sch 21(s269) of the CJA 2003. When considering the sentence, the presiding judge, Mr Justice Treacy, relied on *R v Stapley* (2004), where the sentencing judge in that case took the view that when considering the appropriate sentence for conspiracy to murder, the court should have regard to the guidelines in terms of recommended minimum terms to be served in cases of murder. Gunn, Russell and McNee appealed and the case was heard by the Court of Appeal Criminal Division on 3 May 2007. Sir Igor Judge for the Appeal Court summed up thus:

> "In our judgement when assessing the determinate sentence the judge was not obliged by statute to have regard to the principles set out in Schedule 21. There are no words of obligation. However, we fully endorse his decision to do so as entirely logical and an inevitable consequence of the new regime for sentencing in cases of murder."

The appeals were dismissed (EWCA Crim 1529).

SETTING THE MINIMUM TERM FOR ATTEMPTED MURDER

The minimum term for attempted murder is currently influenced by Sch 21 principles. Following recent Court of Appeal rulings, in particular that of *R v Kevin Ford* (EWCA Crim 1358) where the sentence was reduced, the Sentencing Guidelines Council (SGC) are consulting widely on minimum terms in relation to attempted murder. In its consultation paper the SGC makes the point that it is necessary to provide sentencing levels in relation to attempted murder that are more obviously linked to the starting points for murder that Parliament has established and contained within the CJA 2003; with the added caveat that 'link' needs to incorporate the level of harm caused as well as the circumstances in which the attempt took place. In other words, the SGC recognise that the range of harm that can result from an attempted murder can be very wide and suggests, for instance, that the starting point where no harm has been caused should result in a time spent in custody of 40% of the minimum term that would have been imposed had the offence been murder.

SETTING THE MINIMUM TERM FOR DISCRETIONARY LIFERS/ IPP

The setting of the tariff in relation to life sentences other than murder is done by the Judge in open court. Provision relating to the setting of the minimum term are contained within s82A of the Powers of Criminal Courts (Sentencing) Act 2000. In the case of discretionary lifers and IPP (a more detailed account of the sentencing of Craig Sweeney to IPP can be found in Chapter 1), the Judge has to decide what fixed-term sentence would have been handed down if a life sentence had not been necessary. The Judge then sets the tariff at between one-half and two-thirds of the equivalent determinate sentence and this period therefore determines when he or she becomes eligible for parole.

A BRIEF NOTE ON APPEALS (MURDER)

Section 271 of the CJA 2003 provides that:

> 'an appeal can be made by an offender, either against the minimum term set by the court in a murder case, or against a decision by that court to set a 'whole life' minimum term. Of course there can be no appeal against a mandatory sentence as such but s 271(1) inserts a new sub section (1A) into s 9 of the Criminal Appeal Act 1968 to make it clear that an appeal may lie against the minimum term set by the court.'

> (Taylor, Wasik and Leng, 2004)

The Attorney General can, under ss 35 and 36 of the CJA 1988 (Reviews of Sentencing), refer a minimum term in a murder case to the Court of Appeal if he believes the sentence was unduly lenient. Such an appeal was raised by the Attorney General Lord Goldsmith QC in the case of Michael Hamer, who received a 12-year jail term for the murder of Joe Geeling. Three Judges sitting at the Court of Appeal raised the sentence from 12 to 15 years.

PAROLE

The functions of the Parole Board are laid out in Sch 19 to, and s239 of, the CJA 2003.

> 'The Board is given a duty 'to advise the Secretary of State with respect to any matter referred to it by him concerned with the early release or recall

of prisoners. It must, under that section, when dealing with cases in respect of which it makes a recommendation, consider (a) any documents given to it by the Secretary of State and (b) any other oral or written information obtained by it.'

(Gibson, 2004)

Criteria governing the release of life sentence prisoners can be found in the Secretary of State's Directions to the Parole Board (s32(6) of the CJA 1991). There are two types of parole review. The first review is considered on the papers only and should normally begin around three years before the tariff expires or, in cases where a lifer has moved onto a Second Stage Cat. C prison, four and a half years before tariff expiry. In cases of short tariffs, the first review is set by LRRS caseworkers on the basis of tariff length and progress in custody. Some IPP prisoners can have tariffs as short as 18 months and will not usually therefore have a pre-tariff review. In such cases the prisoner is entitled to have a first review shortly before the tariff expiry to consider suitability for release on the expiry date (*LM* para. 5.1.3). The second and subsequent reviews following tariff expiry contain an oral hearing and are often referred to as DLPs (Discretionary Lifer Panels). Prior to January 2004, prisoners serving a mandatory life sentence had access only to a paper review. However, in 2002 the European Court of Human Rights ruled that the procedures in relation to mandatory lifers were a breach of Article 5. As a result of this decision, mandatory lifers who have served the minimum term of their sentence have the right to an oral hearing and the Parole Board can direct their release (*Stafford v UK* (2002)). The powers relating to release can be found in s275 of the CJA 2003.

Timetable

The First Parole Board Review will only consider the prisoner's suitability for transfer to open conditions. The first review date will be notified to the lifer by LRRS with a copy sent to the supervising Offender Manager.

Parole Board Procedures as set out in Chapter 5 of the Lifer Manual:

1. Preliminary stages of pre-tariff review. LRRS discloses skeleton dossier to arrive 15 working days prior to start of review proper. Prison to add complete set of LSP reports to skeleton dossier.

2. Review starts. Complete dossier is disclosed to prisoner. Prisoner has 28 days to make representations.

3. Deadline for prisoner's representations.

4. Prison sends full dossier (including prisoner's representations) to Parole Board.

5. Parole Board considers case.

6. Parole Board notifies LRRS of panel decision.

7. LRRS notifies prisoner of further review in closed conditions (known as knock back decision).

8. LRRS notifies prisoner of acceptance of Parole Board's recommendation for transfer to open conditions.

9. LRRS notifies prisoner of rejection of Board's recommendation for transfer to open conditions and the date of the next review.

Reports

In addition to other reports submitted to the dossier, the supervising Offender Manager and seconded probation officer are required to provide reports (this used to be LSP3E, now it is PAROM1) which must draw upon the OASys assessment prepared by the Offender Manager and, where possible, the OASys document should be made available to Parole Board in the dossier. There is evidence from research carried out by the Home Office on non-lifer parolees that reports written by probation staff are very influential and that there was a 'strong correlation' between the recommendations of both the seconded officer and home supervising officer and the parole decision (Hood & Shute, 2000). It is reasonable to assume therefore that the reports written by probation staff on lifers are no less influential.

Prison establishments need to ensure that they provide the prisoner with a copy of the dossier and access to it as frequently as resources allow. Some documents can be withheld from the prisoner (see para. 6 of the Parole Board Rules), mainly on the grounds of national security, to prevent further crime or disorder, or to safeguard the health and welfare of the prisoner or other. It is for the Chair of the panel to decide whether the material should be withheld from the prisoner and, if so, whether it should be disclosed to the prisoner's legal representative (*LM*, para. 5.9.5). In *Roberts v Parole Board* (2004), the House of Lords endorsed the Parole Board's action in disclosing highly sensitive information to a special advocate lawyer rather than the legal representative of the prisoner, so as to protect the source of the information (*Parole Board Report*, 05/06).

Parole Member Interviews

Prior to April 2004, prisoners were interviewed by a Parole Board member before the paper parole panel hearing. For paper panels this was the only opportunity for someone from the Parole Board to meet face-to-face with the prisoner. The majority of the funding for these interviews was withdrawn by the Home Office after it conducted research which questioned the value of the process (Parole Board Report, 05/06). However, the Parole Board has committed itself to re-introducing these interviews from April 2007 onwards. These member interviews will be selectively for offenders who pose a particular concern to the Board, for instance those prisoners convicted of a sexual or violent offence who are recommended for parole by report writers.

Second and Subsequent Reviews or DLPs

The purpose of the review is to consider the prisoner's suitability for release. The priority consideration for release is that it is no longer necessary for the protection of the public for the prisoner to remain in custody.

'The test to be applied by the Parole Board in reaching its decision on release is whether or not the prisoner's level of risk to the life and limb of others is more than minimal. The risk in question is one of serious sexual or violent offending, regardless of the type of index offending. If the Parole Board considers that this test is met, they must direct the prisoner's release on life licence.'

(LM para. 6.1)

In order for the prisoner to be considered for release on tariff expiry, the LRRS will refer the case to the Parole Board.

Parole Board Procedures

1. The Parole Board lists the case and notifies the prisoner and the LRRS of the oral hearing date.

2. The LRRS discloses the skeleton dossier and the prisoner informs the Parole Board of details of legal representative.

3. The Prison discloses the complete dossier to the prisoner, the Parole Board and the LRRS.

4. Prisoner sends representations and independent reports to the Parole Board and the LRRS.

5. A single Parole Board member considers the case and makes the decision.

6. The decision of the single member is notified to parties.

7. If the decision is not to release, the lifer notifies the Parole Board and LRRS that a three-member panel oral hearing is required. If no oral hearing is required, the provisional decision by the single member becomes final. If an oral hearing is required, parties submit written application to the Parole Board and each other with witness attendance details and evidence. An oral hearing will then take place not later than 26 weeks after the commencement of review.

8. If the decision of the single member is to refer the case for oral hearing, the decision is notified to parties; each party then submits written applications to the Parole Board and an oral hearing takes place no longer than 26 weeks after the commencement of review.

9. If the decision of the single member is in favour of release, this is referred to a three-member panel for consideration and their decision is notified to all parties. If an oral hearing is required then parties submit written applications to the Parole Board. The oral hearing is held no longer than 26 weeks after the commencement of proceedings. The panel's decision is then provided in writing to all concerned parties within seven days of the hearing.

Reports

As in the case of the first review, the supervising Offender Manager and seconded probation officer will be required to submit an LSP3E using all risk assessment documentation, especially OASys. The procedure for withholding information remains the same as in the First Review.

The Hearing

An oral hearing, normally at the lifer's establishment, will always be held unless the prisoner and the Home Secretary, together with the panel chairperson, agree otherwise, even in the unlikely event that the prisoner opts not to attend the hearing. If the prisoner declines to appear or to be represented, the review will almost certainly be based simply on the written reports and be held at the Parole Board's premises.

The formal 'parties' at the hearing are the prisoner and the Home Secretary. Prisoners may represent themselves but are entitled to be represented. Legal Aid is available to secure representation by a solicitor who may, in turn, instruct a barrister: however, the representative does not have to be a lawyer (although neither a serving prisoner or someone with an unspent criminal conviction can act in this capacity). If a prisoner does not authorise representation, the Board may, with the prisoner's agreement, appoint someone to act on his/her behalf. The Home Office's case is presented by the Lifer Liaison Officer of the holding prison who will also have submitted a report on the prisoner. Where the LLO's report expresses a view which conflicts with the Home Secretary's stance, another governor will normally present the case instead to avoid conflict of interest.

Attendance by Probation Officers and Observers

Although the hearing is held in private and information about the proceedings should not be made public, the chairperson may admit as an observer anyone they consider appropriate. The supervising Offender Manager is expected to attend and the prisoner in any event can, under Rule 7, ask the supervising Offender Manager to attend as a witness. Offender Managers can contribute greatly to the process through knowledge of the intended release area, victims' issues, applications to Approved Premises and, most crucially, through knowledge gained having carried out a full risk assessment using OASys. Adequate preparation time should be built into an Offender Manager's workload management as well as time spent on attendance. Oral hearings may last up to a day or as little as a few minutes but typically extend for 1–2 hours.

DECISIONS TO RELEASE

The case of Anthony Rice who murdered Naomi Bryant whilst on life licence received much news coverage at a time when the sentencing of other offenders, not all of whom were subject to licence as in the case of Craig Sweeney, was very much in the public spotlight. The *Observer* newspaper, commenting on this pressure reported comments made by the Lord Chief Justice Lord Phillips to a 'behind-closed-doors-briefing to the All-Party Parliamentary Penal Affairs Group', where he is alleged to have told the audience that the CJA 2003 had created new pressures for 'both the parole board and the probation service' by allowing a populist agenda to potentially skew the judicial process (*The Observer*, 18 June 2006).

Professor Sir Duncan Nichol CBE, in his role as Chairman of the Parole Board, reacted to the debate writing as follows:

'A lot has been written recently about human rights and how they are supposedly undermining public protection considerations. With regard to the Board this agenda has been misrepresented and consistently overplayed by the media. Our members are very well aware that their overriding consideration should not be for the rights of the prisoner, but public safety and that concern over the possibility of a judicial review should be subordinate to concerns about the risk of harm a prisoner might pose.'

(Parole Board Annual Report, 05/06)

The statistics for release by the Parole Board of mandatory life sentences in 2005/06 showed, out of 249 cases considered, 37 (equal to 15%) were recommended for release – the lowest for five years. Paul Cavadino, Chief Executive of Nacro, commented:

'Public safety must be paramount in parole decisions. However, it would be regrettable if the pendulum swung too far under media or political pressure and to prisoners who could safely be released under supervision remaining inside'.

(Nacro Press Release, 6 November 2006)

If the Parole Board make a recommendation for release, it follows that that direction is binding on the Secretary of State. Should release not be directed, LRRS will consider any recommendations made regarding open conditions and will set the date of the next review. There is no right of appeal against a parole decision except by way of judicial review.

8
LIFE LICENCE AND RECALL

Life sentence prisoners can only be released once their tariff date has expired and at the direction of the Parole Board. Legislation governing the release of lifers serving IPP sentences is contained within Sch 18 to, and s230 of, the Criminal Justice Act 2003. Provision relating to the release of other lifers is covered by s28(5) of the Crime (Sentences) Act 1997.

ACTION UPON AUTHORISATION OF RELEASE

The Parole Board notifies LRRS of the direction to release. LRRS contact the Lifer Manager at the prison and the supervising Offender Manager to inform them of the release direction and any extra licence conditions recommended by the Parole Board, to request a map (where appropriate) from the Offender Manager outlining any exclusion zones and to discuss a release date.

Once the release date is set, LRRS will send, to the District ACO of the intended release area, a copy of the licence and information about any aspects or issues the Probation Service should be aware of plus a copy of the dossier submitted to the Parole Board review that resulted in the release. A date for the first risk assessment or progress report will also be sent at the same time. The ACO must then pass these copies on to the Offender Manager. During HMIP's inquiry into the circumstances of the death of John Monckton, they discovered that there existed little clarity about who held responsibility for reviewing a decision when an offenders circumstances change between the decision to release and the actual release. In their findings, the Inspectorate recommended that the Parole Board should specify what should happen in situations where release is dependent on a requirement which in practice cannot be met (Probation Circular 15/2006).

Notification to the Police

Immediately on the lifer's release, LRRS will notify the National Identification Service (NIS) at New Scotland Yard (and the relevant Chief Constable if outside the Metropolitan Police District) of the address at which the lifer proposes to live. The supervising Offender Manager, through the Assistant Chief Officer, should notify the NIS and Chief Constable of all subsequent changes of address. LRRS will inform the NIS when supervision conditions have been removed or the life licensee dies.

Prior to release, liaison between the supervising Probation Area and local police is essential, sharing information and details of licence conditions in line with the Joint National Protocol's minimum standards.

Offences against Children

For lifers convicted of offences against children or young persons under the age of 18, the procedures specified in *IG54/1994* should be followed so that the Social Services Department concerned can consider the implications of release for the protection of children and young persons and can take such steps as may be necessary to safeguard any children or young persons who may be placed at risk. Notification should take place at least six weeks before release. The views of Social Services in this respect should have already been obtained when a lifer (who is a CYPA 1933 Sch 1 offender) is being considered for temporary release, transfer to open conditions or placement in Approved Premises or a resettlement prison.

LICENCE CONDITIONS

A life licence authorises the prisoner's release within 15 days of the date of issue. Licences issued before 16 May 2005 contain the standard six conditions. The seventh condition, relating to good behaviour, was added to the licence of prisoners released on or after that date. The seven conditions are:

1. To place himself/herself under the supervision of whichever Offender Manager is nominated for this purpose.

2. To report to the nominated Offender Manager on release and keep in touch with that officer in accordance with that officer's instructions.

3. Receive visits from that officer where the licensee is living, if the Offender Manager so requires.

4. Reside only where approved by the Offender Manager.

5. Work only where approved by the Offender Manager.

6. To refrain from travelling outside the UK without prior permission of the Offender Manager.

7. Be well-behaved and not do anything which could undermine the purpose of supervision on licence which is to protect the public and to secure successful reintegration into community.

These conditions are included in a life licence to ensure the continued safety of the public by providing a continuous assessment of the risk the licensee presents and to facilitate reintegration into the community. Any additional licence conditions can only be inserted if they are lawful. To be lawful the condition has to be necessary and proportionate (PC 16/2005, para. 28).

EXCLUSION ZONES

Conditions relating to the imposition of exclusion zones need to be necessary, reasonable and proportionate. 'Necessary' means that no other means of managing a particular risk is available or appropriate; and 'proportionate' means that the restriction on the offender's liberty is the minimum required to manage the risk (Probation Circular 15/06). In 2002 Stephen Craven, who had been jailed for the murder of a 19-year-old girl in a nightclub in 1991, challenged a condition of his life licence not to enter Newcastle or North Tyneside without the prior permission of his supervising officer. This meant in reality that he had to live away from his family and could not work within the area. Despite the Home Secretary agreeing to a significant reduction in the exclusion zone to enable Mr Craven to visit his parents by private transport and using main roads, the case was taken to Judicial Review. The Court found that although Mr Craven's right under Article 8 of the European Convention to a family life had been restricted, such restriction in this case was proportionate and necessary to protect the victim's family who still lived in the area (*R (Craven) v Secretary of State for the Home Department and the Parole Board* (2002)).

The exclusion zone should be specific and the offender must have no doubt as to the boundaries of the zone. Entry into the zone can only be granted by the Offender Manager. The Offender Manager should ensure that the offender is not required to report to Probation Office or other facility within the zone unless there are exceptional circumstances. Practice guidance contained within Probation Circular 15/06 specifies:

> 'The supervising officer should seek to avoid issuing reporting instructions within the exclusion area unless they are agreed and recorded in advance by a senior manager at ACO level or equivalent. In terms of the probation office or treatment provider being located within the exclusion zone, and where the exclusion reflects a request from victims, the Victims Liaison Officer should be informed as to the precise time and date of the offender's attendance at the location within the exclusion zone. The consequences of the offender not adhering to the set appointments and the times at which they are permitted within the exclusion zone should be clearly spelt out and reinforced.'

Contact with the Licensee

The supervision of all offenders released on licence, including life licence, is covered by the criteria laid out in the National Standards for the Management of Offenders 2007. Lifers will be located at Tier 4 and, as such, will be seen on the day of the release by the Offender Manager. A second contact has to be arranged to take place within three working days of release. A home visit has to be undertaken within ten working days of release and contact is to be at least once weekly. Subsequent risk reviews may indicate that the lifer can be managed at Tier 3.

REPORTS TO THE HOME OFFICE

The Lifer Team within LRRS (Post-Release Team) requires periodic reports about the licensee's progress. The reports should be informed by a recently completed OASys and the first report must be submitted one month after release and then reports will expected on a quarterly basis for the first two years. At this point, LRRS will consider whether it is possible to reduce the need for reports to every six or twelve months. The frequency of progress reports should not be confused with the frequency of licensee reporting to the Offender Manager supervising the licence. All reports should be endorsed by an ACO, whose comments should be added, especially where the Offender Manager has recommended a particular course of action – be it variations of the licence or recall.

Progress reports should contain sufficient relevant information to enable the Lifer Team at LRRS to determine whether or not the licensee presents an acceptable risk to remain in the community. There is a standard template for the progress report which can be found at Annexe F of PC 29/2007 'Post Release Enforcement – Licence Conditions'.

In addition, reports should always be submitted to LRRS in any of the following circumstances (*LM* para. 13.15):

- if it appears likely that the safety of the public may be at risk;

- if the Offender Manager loses touch with the licensee;

- if there has been a breach of conditions of the licence;

- if the licensee's behaviour suggests that further serious offences may be committed;

- if the licensee has been charged with any offence (with full details of the nature of the charge);

- if the licensee's domestic circumstances appear to be unsatisfactory;

- if there are any significant changes in the licensee's personal relationship (*eg* marriage, co-habitation, breakdown of relationships, arrival of children), especially where such changes relate in any way to the original offence;

- if the licensee's mental condition gives cause for concern; or

- if the licensee's behaviour or activities are likely to give rise to media attention.

TRAVEL ABROAD
Residence Abroad
LM para. 13.14.2 specifies:

'Life licensees or those released after serving a sentence of IPP are not generally released direct from prison to live abroad, as this would contravene the requirement for supervision after release. Any licensee requesting to live permanently abroad will only receive approval after a thorough risk assessment and agreement of the ACCO and LRRS. Licensees will need to demonstrate that they have successfully adjusted to living in the community. Evidence should also be provided to show that the country the licensee is travelling to is aware of the life licensee's status and intention to reside there.'

The manual goes on to comment that each case will be considered on its individual merits.

Temporary Absence Abroad
Approval to travel abroad for short periods, including holidays, is at the discretion of the District ACO in the licensee's area. They must be satisfied that the licensee may be trusted to return. Any doubt should equate to refusal and, if necessary, further liaison with the LRRS. *LM* para. 13.14 specifies that 'There is no minimum period of supervision required following release before such an application would be entertained'. As with residence abroad, each case is considered on its merits. Prior to travelling abroad, the Lifer Team of the Post Release Section require notification of the country or countries to be visited, dates and purpose of travel and confirmation of whether permission has been granted (PC 29/2007).

CANCELLATION OF SUPERVISION
LM para. 13.9.2 specifies that consideration can be given to cancellation of the supervision element of the life licence, including those on IPP licence, after a minimum of 'four years of trouble-free existence in the community'. However, for lifers convicted of sex offences released on life/IPP licence, cancellation will not usually be considered before ten years has elapsed (Sch 18, CJA 2003). Licence conditions can be re-imposed by LRRS should the Probation Area or the police be made aware of any incident involving the lifer. It is thus important that case records are retained for the rest of the licensee's life in case circumstances alter and further statutory responsibilities arise.

"PC 29/2007 stipulates that cancellation of the supervision element of an indeterminate licence requires evidence of:

89

- a stable lifestyle, good integration, a balanced outlook and an open relationship with the Offender Manager;

- gradual reduction in the requirement for contact with the Probation Area;

- crises, if any, having been faced and dealt with sensibly, with proper involvement of the Offender Manager and;

- where appropriate, an indication that the licensee would turn to the Probation Area for assistance on a voluntary basis if necessary"(PC 29/2007, p9).

THE REALITY OF LICENCE

Coker and Martin (1985) provide the most detailed – if somewhat dated – account of the realities of life licence available to lifers and their probation officers. Two cohorts were studied: the 64 men released in the period 1960–64 and the 175 men released in the period 1970–74, totalling 239; 192 being convicted of murder. To gain greater depth of knowledge of the experience of supervision, interviews were conducted with 33 men released in 1974 and their most recent supervising officers.

Reconviction History

Starting with the most stark factor in assessing the success of licence, Coker and Martin found that in a varying follow-up period from 5 to 19 years, depending on the date of the lifer's release, 65 (27%) of the total sample were re-convicted, 20 (31%) re-offending within a year of release and 34 (53%) in less than 2 years. Given that 62% of the sample had criminal convictions before their life sentence, this represented a considerable improvement on their previous records. 25 of the men (10%) committed serious offences; 15 involving violence, ranging from manslaughter (2 instances) to fighting outside a pub, in 8 instances involving a woman victim. (In 114 cases, women had been the victim of the life sentence offence.) 11 of the 15 men who committed a serious violent offence had no previous convictions for violence except their life sentence crime. 24 out of 28 men with a previous record of serious violence in addition to their life crime did not repeat that sort of crime. 30 of the 65 re-offenders committed only non-violent petty crime.

Age

Of 40 men aged 50 or over on release, only one was convicted of a further offence of any kind but of 85 men aged in their 40s on release, half were convicted of a further offence, albeit that nearly 70% of their crimes were non-violent. Re-offending involving serious violence was not age-specific and occurred across the age range of those aged under 60 on release.

Duration of Supervision

Taking Coker and Martin's second cohort as a more reliable indicator of recent experience, and excluding 7 men who were deported, 126 (75%) of the sample had made good progress and their supervision had been discharged within 5 years of their release. 12 were back in prison or special hospital after recall. Of the remaining 30 men, 2 were being sought by the police following issue of warrants for their arrest and 11 had been re-released following earlier recall. Thus only 17 (10%) remained on continuous supervision beyond 5 years.

Factors associated with prolonged supervision were primarily issues of public safety and concern about risk, arising from (i) the nature of the life offence (particularly if this involved 'psychological abnormality'), (ii) the licensee's record of convictions for serious violence prior to their life sentence, and/or (iii) alarming behaviour on licence which concerned the supervisor. Nearly 40% of lifers whose crime had been sexual and 68% of men having pre-life sentence convictions for serious violence were supervised for more than five years.

In some instances, licensees continued to be supervised for no clear reason, where the men concerned appeared to be socially, personally and economically settled. Coker speculates that this might arise because of 'administrative inertia' or because of 'something intangible in a man's circumstances about which the authorities needed to feel the reassurance provided by time'. Mr AP illustrated caution of the latter kind. Though he had worked and behaved well throughout and had received no unfavourable reports, he displayed an aggressive dislike of supervision which he regarded as an irrelevant irritation. He had acquired seven convictions prior to his life sentence for manslaughter of a man killed in a pub brawl and had returned on licence to his home area where he was affiliated to the criminal sub-culture in a district with a high crime rate. His previous record and his hostile demeanour suggested the continuance of his supervision as a precaution.

Prolonged supervision did not necessarily denote risk or lack of success but might reflect the belief that it provided 'a reassuring stability' or necessary support for the lifer. Men aged 50 or older on release did not necessarily spend less time on supervision and this appeared linked in many instances to their comparative social isolation, their supervisor's wish to alleviate their loneliness and their positive appreciation of supervisory attention. Shorter periods of supervision were commonly experienced by (a) men who were under 40 on release and who stood the best chance of re-establishing themselves, and (b) the elderly who presented minimum threat to the public.

Experience of Supervision

From an admittedly small sample of lifers interviewed, 24 out of 33 viewed supervision negatively, though their criticisms applied primarily to the system rather than to their probation officer. They accepted the routine demand as the price to be paid for their freedom.

In summary:

> 'The men regarded supervision as unnecessary to their resettlement and a hindrance to their peace of mind but they had learned to conform in prison and complied in varying degrees in spite of their feelings about supervision.'

Only half of the sample thought weekly reporting was essential or desirable, even in the early days of licence, but despite this reluctance, 'many adjusted to it and tried to capitalise on its inevitability'. There was no evidence that men who expressed resentment to being supervised fared differently in their resettlement from the remainder.

Of the quarter of the sample who spoke positively of supervision, comments ranged from 'If (the probation officer) said jump, I'd have said 'how high?'' to 'the probation officer had more problems than me'. It was not possible to identify social factors which may have prompted positive regard; personal characteristics such as anxiety, conformity or guilt which might have been significant could not be measured.

Two-thirds of the lifers perceived surveillance as the central function of supervision but 8 (24%) saw the social work possibilities as the most important. Overall, about three-quarters of the sample were prepared to acknowledge that they suffered some problem on discharge; these were emotional rather than practical and were associated with self-confidence.

> 'Whereas in prison they had been accepted and even been members of an elite, outside they were again responsible for themselves, knowing themselves to be lifers, always liable to be suspect and viewed askance by anyone learning of their status. Inevitably they carried potential feelings of alienation which they had to learn how to handle.'

(Coker and Martin, 1985).

There was little evidence that such uncomfortable feelings were discussed with their probation officers and lifers were well aware that if they were too ready to disclose their fears, 'this might have involved the risk of arousing official anxiety with its inherent possibility of jeopardising their freedom'. It frequently felt too risky to reveal to the probation officer anxieties about any inability to cope because, once disclosed, the lifer had no way of knowing what would become of the information, how it would be interpreted, or what effect it would have upon his position. Officers often showed a good understanding in the face of the men's desire to keep many of their immediate post-release problems to themselves. Coker and Martin comment:

> 'The style of supervision suggested by this research is that which accords the lifer as much trust and dignity as possible within the framework of the licence requirements. This depends on a realisation of the importance and inevitability of self-determination and self-control, as well as of the lifer's need to strike out independently and to cast off his prison label and identity ... Without exception the interviewed men stated unequivocally that they were responsible for their own behaviour; they wanted to be treated as individuals and not treated as cases. Such an approach does not exclude a firm insistence on compliance with the conditions of licence. Nevertheless, men recognised the value of a fair and sympathetic listener with whom they might discuss, if they chose, some of their affairs. Probation officers must learn the importance of 'being' rather than 'doing'.'

New Relationships

Since many men in the research cohorts (43%) had received life for killing a woman, any new relationship formed after release was bound to raise their supervisor's anxieties. 27 (63%) of the 43 men who had killed a partner remarried or were cohabiting within 5 years of their release. Men who had killed other women (and who might therefore still have had a wife to whom they could return) had an even higher rate (81%) of establishing or re-establishing a matrimonial or co-habitational home. In contrast, men who were single or unattached at the time of their life offence, whether they had killed a woman or not, were far less likely to marry or co-habit after their release – only 41% compared with 75% for those married or co-habiting at the time of their offence.

It was often difficult for the supervising probation officer to judge the quality of the new relationship without risking invasion of privacy or prying. Men in the smaller sub-sample of 33 interviewed were equally divided as to whether their supervisor should see their spouse or girlfriend. Though a quarter of the sub-sample indicated that they were prepared to tell the probation officer 'anything s/he wanted to know', this appeared to be a qualified affirmative, as illustrated by the man who commented 'I tend to be open, unless it's really bad like'. Probation officers felt that this area of a man's life could legitimately be invaded 'by the subterfuge of a friendly relationship' but, 'faced with difficulties of assessing dangerous men in such intimate settings', they 'opted for caution'. As an illustration of the problems of balancing intangibles and uncertainties in predicting risk, where caution finally prevailed, a man who had established a *ménage à trois* was recalled because of official qualms about the risk presented by this unusual relationship.

Reconviction Statistics

A Home Office research study published in 1997 looked at the reconviction rates of offenders released on life licence for the first time between 1972 and 1994 (Kershaw, Dowdswell & Goodman, 1997). Of the 1,691 lifers released, 362 were reconvicted following the commission of a standard list offence and 66 were convicted of a grave offence (*ie* homicide, serious wounding, rape, buggery, robbery, aggravated burglary and arson). The reconviction rates for standard list offences for life licensees were much lower than the average for all those released from custody. The most common offences on reconviction (within 2 years of release) were theft and handling (45% of convictions), with violence against the person accounting for 22% and burglary 13%. Reconviction rates for those without previous convictions were half of those licensees who had previous convictions.

21 licensees in the sample were reconvicted for homicide and received a further life sentence – of these, 19 had an index offence of homicide. The reconviction rates for mandatory life licensees were slightly lower than for discretionary lifers.

Power of Recall

The Secretary of State can revoke a life licence at any time (s32(1) of the Crime (Sentences) Act 1997) on the recommendation of the Parole Board. Between 1 April 2006 and September 2006, a total of 85 life licensees had been recalled to prison. Of the 140 determinate sentence offenders recalled to prison in 05/06, 87 were recalled for committing further offences, 8 for being out of touch with their supervising officer, 19 for failing to reside as directed and 26 for 'other reasons' (Parole Board, 06).

Risk of Recall

Managing risk and protecting the public are at the heart of what the Probation Service does. Along with 'professional wisdom'; however, there are a plethora of tools available to assess risk: OASys, SARA (Spousal, Assault, Reconviction, Assessment) and Risk Matrix 2000 for example, and multi-agency working through MAPPA (Multi-Agency Public Protection Arrangements) risk management will always remain an inexact science.

A study of 118 lifers released in the first 5 years of the DLP (Discretionary Lifer Panel) process between 1992 and 1997 identified 13 characteristics strongly associated with a higher risk of recall:

(i)   misused alcohol following the first DLP release;

(ii)   having a higher number of previous convictions;

(iii)   having been 18 years of age or below at the time of first conviction;

(iv) scoring 25 or more on the PCL-R;

(v) having no psychological problems at the time of the offence;

(vi) being sexually motivated at the time of the index offence;

(vii) not knowing the victim of the index offence;

(viii) experiencing local authority care during childhood;

(ix) having been abused during childhood;

(x) having committed an index offence which included a sexual element;

(xi) using alcohol as a disinhibitor for the index offence;

(xii) having been hostile to the home probation officer during custody; and

(xiii) having mental health problems on release.

(Home Office, 2005)

The authors of the study went on to acknowledge that, whilst it was difficult to quantify the level and standard of probation supervision before and after release from custody, the analysis indicated that lifers who received extensive contact during the custodial period were less likely to be recalled. However, interestingly enough, they felt that this difference was not statistically significant.

Recommendation for Recall
LM para. 13.19 specifies:

> 'It has to be shown that there is a risk of danger to the public before recall is likely to be agreed. The supervising Probation Area must take into account the extent that the licensee's behaviour presents a risk of sexual or violent harm to others, regardless of the type of index offence for which he or she was originally convicted.'

RECALL TO PRISON

> 'Recall frequently involves sentencing someone for something they have not yet done but which it is feared they might do. The burden of proof is effectively on the prisoner.'

> 'Such a process clearly requires the most stringent application of the principles of fairness. Those to whom it applies have already served the period of imprisonment deemed to be sufficient as punishment, and have been assessed as posing no further risk to society. There should therefore be powerful, and challengeable, reasons for re-detention.'

'Justice' (1996b)

'I don't really care if I'm recalled to prison. Being inside has got no fears for me. In my mind I'm a prisoner whether I'm inside or not.'

'Philip Derbyshire' in Parker (1990)

Recall is a sanction of considerable gravity, returning the lifer to custody for an indefinite period, whether intended as a short lesson or a return to square one of risk assessment, sometimes a decision made on the clearest of grounds but on occasion on rather sparse or ambiguous information, sometimes after very careful and considered reflection but at other times against the clock. As Coker and Martin (1985) note, recall serves 'both as a precaution and a penalty', with the public interest as the paramount consideration, albeit with the lifer's resettlement needs and progress also in mind. Of 578 lifers released in the period 1990–1995, 37 (6.4%) had been recalled by June 1996 (Parliamentary written answer 17 June 1996).

Unless supervision has been suspended (see page 89), a recall decision will almost certainly involve the supervising Offender Manager either as the initiator of concern or in giving information, advice or a recommendation. As Coker and Martin observe, to request a prisoner's recall is an exercise of power requiring one of the most difficult professional judgments that an Offender Manager has to make. An aggrieved recalled lifer may opt not only to use statutory channels to challenge the validity of their recall but may also pursue a complaint against the probation officers concerned under Probation Service complaints procedures.

Lifers are often worried that they may be recalled for trivial reasons or because of ungrounded fears of suspicions. But revocation should not be based on arbitrary whim. The critical test in law is whether the decision is 'rational' in balancing competing considerations of risk and liberty: *R v Secretary of State, ex parte Macneill* (1994) *The Times*, 26 May. Recall may nevertheless be based not on 'first hand' evidence but on the basis of probation reports relaying hearsay allegations. 'Justice' (1996b) gives the example of a mandatory lifer, originally convicted of the murder of his wife, who was recalled on the grounds that he had mistreated and hit a woman with multiple sclerosis whom he had befriended. This came about because of allegations by various people such as a home help, even though the woman herself denied the allegations.

Further Offence or Alleged Offence

Though a licence 'would not normally be revoked if the licensee had committed a minor offence unrelated to that which led to his life licence', Annual Reports of the Parole Board refer to recall following a wide range of offences including conspiracy to murder and robbery at the more serious end of the spectrum to actual bodily harm, 'breach of the peace' and 'driving offences', though it is not possible to identify if the licensee committing less serious offences also presented other cause for concern.

If the cause for concern centres on criminal behaviour, will recall be 'rational' only if the licensee has been *convicted* of a further offence? In *ex parte Macneill* (see above) a mandatory lifer had been charged with affray while on licence and sought judicial review claiming that revocation of the licence following committal proceedings but prior to trial and conviction was contrary to the presumption of innocence. Rejecting his application, Staughton LJ stated that the Home Secretary is entitled to act on evidence of criminal activity by a licensee regardless of whether s/he had been tried or could be tried for an offence. The Divisional Court noted that the licensee had not denied the affray nor raised a defence and at the Crown Court had raised the question whether a trial was now necessary in view of the intervening revocation. The affray charge was subsequently ordered to 'lie on the file'. The licensee had access to the prosecution depositions and was thus fully aware of the adverse material against him and had accepted that an acquittal would not lead to the automatic restoration of licence.

Though recall was clearly rational in this instance, *ex parte Macneill* raises the possibility that mere accusation of any criminal offence will not necessarily provide rational grounds for revocation, for example if the offence is of a very minor nature, *eg* simple possession of a small amount of cannabis for personal use, or a defence is clearly asserted, particularly if the licensee's behaviour is in other respects satisfactory. Further judicial review proceedings will no doubt seek to test this issue. 'Justice' (1996b) has suggested that the court might feel obliged to hold differently in the case of a discretionary lifer in the same position as Mr Macneill.

Commission of a further offence does not automatically trigger recall. Among Coker's sample of released lifers (see page 90), 65 re-offended of whom 27 (42%) were recalled. Not surprisingly, the commission of 'serious violence' (*ie* actual violence or threats leading to a prison sentence) led to recall in all 15 instances but only five out of ten licensees who had committed 'serious non-violent' offences for which they received prison terms were recalled, though the researchers caution that it would be unwise to assume that the 50% rate would be found with a larger sample. It should also be noted that some offences categorised as 'non-violent' nevertheless had features suggestive of potential violence. For example, a man who had completed 12 years on life licence was convicted of two offences of commercial burglary, committed within two months of each other, in one of which a table leg had been unscrewed for possible use as a weapon. Though given a suspended sentence for the new offences, his licence was revoked because of some similarity to his original offence in which he had hit a night security guard with a hammer during an attempted robbery. Of 40 minor offenders only seven were recalled and 'it seems likely that ... their petty crime was also accompanied by behaviour causing concern to their probation officer'. As Coker's research was undertaken before 1980, it should not be assumed to reflect contemporary recall policy.

Violations and Other Concerns

Only eight men in Coker's sample were reported for violations of the terms of their licence, seven being recalled. In contrast, one in three of the sample gave their probation officers sufficient grounds for concern for them to submit a report to the Home Office. 'Whether this was a precautionary act on the officer's part or whether it reflected a natural anxiety that no chances should be taken, is difficult to tell.' Out of 65 men reported as subject of concern, only 19 (29%) had their licences revoked. Among instances of men recalled on this ground:

> 'Mr E, because of excessive drinking and generally unstable behaviour, as reflected by his wife's complaints against him. She was also a heavy drinker and they fought when both were drunk.'

> 'Mr G, who had received life for shooting a man who made a noise in the street, after family complaints led to the discovery of weapons in his bedroom.'

In current practice, for the Board to have sufficient grounds for grave concern to justify recommendation of recall, a breach of the licence needs to be established. Otherwise, the Board would be likely to be found to have acted 'unreasonably' in an application for judicial review (personal communication by the Secretary of the Parole Board, 1996).

THE RECALL PROCESS

There are two types of recall to be considered if a life licensee (including IPP) presents an unacceptable risk to the public: emergency and standard.

Emergency

The procedures for an emergency recall under s32(2) of the Crime Sentences Act 1997 should be followed where a licensee presents an immediate risk to public safety and recall action needs to be instigated by LRRS as a matter of urgency (that risk doesn't have to be based on the licensee being charged with a criminal offence). In such cases there is not time to contact the Parole Board for advice prior to recall action. Emergency recall action will be appropriate in cases where the licensee's behaviour presents an immediate risk of sexual or violent harm to others, regardless of the type of index offence for which the licensee was originally charged.

Standard

Recalls under s32(1) – standard – should take place where there are concerns that the licensee presents an unacceptable risk to the public: however, the circumstances of the case allows LRRS the time to refer the case to the Parole Board for advice on recall action. The Probation Service should discuss a potential recall case with LRRS (Post-Release Team) in the first instance and then submit a written recall request which needs to be endorsed by a ACO. Standard recall may be appropriate in the following examples:

(i)   where there has been persistent breach of licence conditions;

(ii) where there is a long-standing cause for concern for which other measures *eg* warning letters and/or offending behaviour work in the community, have been ineffective;

(iii) where the licensee is out of contact with the Probation Service and the level of risk presented cannot therefore be measured (*Lifer News*).

In the case of lifers released on licence from hospital, they will be subject to recall to prison rather than hospital. The Home Office Mental Health Unit and medical staff at the receiving prison will then consider any transfer back to hospital under ss 47 and 49 of the Mental Health Act 1983.

Representations against Recall

All life sentenced prisoners are entitled to an oral parole hearing to determine if the recall is necessary. Representations made by the licensee should be made available to the Probation Service. The supervising Offender Manager should prepare themselves to attend the oral hearing because there is an expectation of attendance, if not from the Offender Manager then from another appropriate member of the supervising Probation Area. Any documentation from the licensee's case file may be required by the Parole Board and disclosed to the prisoner's representative should they choose to appoint one. Reports submitted to the Parole Board should cover:

• events leading up to recall;

• subsequent developments;

• current level of risk and how or if this can be managed in the community;

• a fresh release plan regardless of whether the probation service is of the view that it is not in favour of release;

• the proposed extent of supervision if re-release is considered;

as well as any extra conditions that should be imposed should re-release be directed.

If the Parole Board do not authorise immediate release (s32(4)), or a licensee does not wish to make representations, the licensee will remain in custody indefinitely. LRRS will set the date for the next review hearing: in accordance with statutory entitlement, the maximum period that can elapse between reviews is two years.

9
THE VICTIM PERSPECTIVE AND PROBATION PRACTICE

The Victim's Charter, first published in 1990, sets out the standards of service victims could expect from all criminal justice agencies including the Probation Service. Although reference is still made to 'victim's charter' issues, the Victim's Charter was replaced in April 2006 by the Victim's Code of Practice.

The relevant piece of legislation containing the code of practice can be found in the Domestic Violence and Victims Act 2004, which gave the Home Secretary the power to issue a code of practice to victims of crime and to appoint a victims commissioner. Under s32 of the Act, Local Criminal Justice Boards (LCJB) are required to implement a protocol which identifies the agreed roles and responsibilities of each of the key criminal justice agencies from the point of reporting the crime right up to the sentencing.

GENERAL ISSUES
Under the Act, local Probation Boards have responsibilities in relation to the victims of offenders sentenced to 12 months or more for a sexual or violent offence, including mentally disordered offenders, in certain circumstances. These responsibilities as set out under s69(4) of the Act and in the code of practice are summarised below. The Probation Service has a responsibility to:

- The victim of an offender who receives a sentence of imprisonment of 12 months or longer after being convicted of a sexual or violent offence.

- The victim of an offender who is (i) convicted of a sexual or violent offence and receives a restricted hospital order (including an order made under criminal insanity legislation), or (ii) transferred to prison under the Mental Health Act 1983 with a restriction direction; or (iii) receives a hospital and limitation direction. (This only applies where the order or direction is made or the transfer to prison is directed on or after 1 July 2005.)

- Take all reasonable steps to establish whether a victim wishes to make representations about what licence conditions or supervision requirements (where it is a young offender) the offender should be subject to on their release from prison and/or conditions of discharge from hospital and to forward these to those responsible for making decisions about the prisoner's or patient's release.

- Forward any requests for non-disclosure to those responsible for making decisions about the prisoner's or patient's release.

- Pass on any information to the victim about whether the prisoner or patient will be subject to any conditions or requirements in the event of release or discharge. Provide the victim with details of any conditions or requirements which relate to contact with the victim or their family and the date on which any restriction order, limitation direction or restriction direction is to cease to have effect.

- Provide the victim with any other information which it considers appropriate in all the circumstances of the case. Generally, victims will be given information of key stages in an offender's sentence, for example, a move to a lower category prison or a temporary release from prison on licence.

The obligations of Prisons and NOMS under the Act can be summarised as follows:

- NOMS must maintain the Prison Service telephone helpline (0845 758 5112) to ensure that victims have a number to ring if they receive unwanted contact from a prisoner who has been convicted or remanded in custody in respect of relevant criminal conduct, or if they have any concerns about the prisoner's temporary release or final discharge.

- The Probation Service may, as a result of information received from the victim, recommend to the Parole Board or the Secretary of State (as appropriate) that conditions relating to non-contact or exclusion are placed on prisoners' release licences. Governors and Controllers of contracted prisons must ensure that all approved conditions are inserted into release licences and that all associated administrative procedures are meeting victims' needs. In addition, prisons must ensure that this information is passed to the Probation Service so that they can notify the victim.

Prisons must ensure that information about victims and their families, or their views and concerns about a prisoner's temporary or permanent release, is stored securely. As a general rule, information provided by the victim which is pertinent to decisions about the conditions of a prisoner's release will be made available to that prisoner, unless the victim requests that it is not disclosed and the Governor considers that to do so would put the victim or their family at risk of harm or would compromise any duty of confidentiality owed to the victim. Victims who wish their views not to be disclosed to the prisoner can make representations to the Governor/Controller through their Victim Liaison Officer.

The Parole Board is required to:

- Consider any representations that victims have offered to the Probation Service on the conditions to be included in the release licences of prisoners serving sentences subject to consideration by the Parole Board and reflect these considerations in the parole decisions. Conditions relating to him/her should be disclosed to the victim through the Probation Service and, where a licence condition has not been included, the Parole Board should provide an explanation for the non-inclusion.

- Consider any information regarding the victim that relates directly to the current risk presented by a prisoner in the decision as to whether or not release should be granted or recommended, and this consideration should be reflected in the parole decision.

SPECIFIC ISSUES

As Probation Circular 29/2003 specifies, for the purpose of victim contact Probation Areas should consider the victim's family to include the following: parents, brothers, sisters, children and other dependents, carers of victims with physical or mental impairment, partners (heterosexual, gay or lesbian) and others with a close personal relationship to the victim.

Purpose of Contact

Victims' families should be advised that the purpose of contact is to keep them informed about the lifer's progress through the prison system Where a victim dies as a result of criminal conduct or suspected criminal conduct, the police will assign a Family Liaison Officer (FLO) and will provide advice 'for bereaved families and friends following murder and manslaughter'. It is important that the Victim Liaison Officer (VLO) liaises where appropriate with the FLO and it is of equal importance that the victim's family understands the role of the VLO and the Offender Manager, in order to dispel any notion that the Probation Service is 'on the side of the offender'.

A written offer of face-to-face contact should be sent by the VLO within 40 working days of sentence for the first contact, although victims' families may prefer alternative forms of contact, *eg* by telephone. It should be noted that victim's wishes regarding contact must be respected and, ultimately, they must be allowed to decide on their preferred method of contact after the initial interview.

Probation Circular 29/03 advised that the Offender Manager needs to ensure that the lifer is made aware of the victim's family's right to make representations regarding conditions of release.

Paragraph 6.3 specifies that Victim Liaison Officers should take all reasonable steps to inform the victim about decisions taken at key stages throughout the sentence but especially when:

- the prisoner appeals against the sentence (however, this is the primary responsibility of the police);

- the prisoner applies for/is granted Release on Temporary Licence (ROTL);

- the prisoner applies for/is granted a work placement in the community;

- a move to open conditions is being considered;

- a move to a lower security establishment or hospital is being considered or granted;

- the tariff of a life sentence prisoner is set or the tariff is reduced or changed;

- a prisoner absconds from/is returned to prison. (With regards to victims and families of mentally disordered offenders, hospital staff will notify the police of such news but it is important for VLOs to develop links with the Care Team so that they are told about such an occurrence. The Mental Health Unit may also inform the VLO where a restricted patient is known to have escaped but this may not be immediate. Incidents where prisoners abscond for brief periods may not routinely be passed to VLOs.);

- the prisoner is the subject of a MAPPA meeting;

- the lifer becomes eligible for parole;

- the lifer reaches tariff expiry (victims of lifers should be consulted about the offenders possible release arrangements at least five years before tariff expiry);

- the outcome of a parole review;

- the prisoner is recalled to prison;

- appeals have been lodged against recall and the outcome of the appeal;

- the prisoner is remanded in custody or re-released pending the outcome of an appeal against recall;

- the case is being closed and contact ended.

Victim Personal Statement (VPS)

In July 2006, the Criminal Justice Review announced that victims should have the opportunity to put forward their views to the Parole Board in cases where release or transfer to open conditions of certain categories of serious offenders is being considered. The government wanted to introduce a 'victim's voice' in the most serious cases heard by the parole board (Home Office 2006(c)). Victims in this instance are those who have opted into the statutory victim contact scheme and where the offender has been sentenced to 12 months or more for a sexual or violent offence. Where the victim died as a result of the offence, a representative of the family is able to submit a Victim Personal Statement (VPS). The VPS should include the views of the victims family about the original impact of the offence and any ongoing consequences along with the likely impact of the offender's release or transfer on those who were close to the victim. The VPS can be submitted to both oral and paper-based hearings.

- For paper hearings, the VPS will be submitted as a written statement which will be considered alongside the other papers.

- Where a case proceeds to an oral hearing, the victim's family representative may request that the statement is made by oral submission. This will normally be presented by a member of the NOMS Public Protection Advocacy Team. In the event of an application by the representative to present the statement personally, the procedures set out in the Parole Board rules will apply (PC 27/2007).

VICTIMS' ADVOCATES SCHEMES

Victims and their families may be dismayed by the relative brevity of a trial where a guilty plea is entered. Brown *et al* (1990) noted murder hearings lasting as little as 20 minutes left families angry 'that their relative was only worth such a short public acknowledgement of their violent death' or that 'the victim became almost inconsequential'. Media reports of the case may have caused additional distress. The end of prosecution proceedings or the initiation of post-sentence contact in homicide cases can often coincide with significant anniversaries, either of the death or of birthdays or wedding anniversaries. Brown *et al* found the families of homicide victims had only just begun gradual resumption of their social activities and contacts 18 months on from their relative's death.

In April 2005, the Government introduced a pilot scheme called the Victims' Advocates Scheme in five courts across the country: the Old Bailey in London, Birmingham Crown Court, Cardiff Crown Court, Manchester Crown Court and Winchester Crown Court. The aim of the scheme is to improve the experience of relatives in two major ways:

1. Ensuring that relatives in murder and manslaughter cases are listened to in court by enabling them to present their views (in person if they choose), after conviction and before sentence, about how the death has affected them.

2. Providing appropriate support to relatives outside of the court throughout the criminal process, including the provision of better information to them by keeping them fully informed of the progress of the prosecution.

The scheme allows those affected to make a Family Impact Statement (FIS), which can be delivered as either:

- a written statement which is given to the judge to read rather than spoken aloud in court;

- an oral statement whereby the court can be addressed by those affected directly, with the help of a CPS lawyer or independent lawyer;

- the CPS prosecutor, an independent lawyer or a lay person can read the FIS in court on behalf of those directly affected.

The FLO will ask a member of the family if they want to make a FIS and how they would like it to be presented. The FLO will pass this on to the CPS and the presiding judge will consider the application. The FIS will be shown to the judge, the defence and the prosecution prior to sentencing and will only be heard in court after conviction and before sentencing.

In the first 11 months of operation some 21 families had made use of the scheme and, on 1 March 2007, Constitutional Affairs Minister Harriet Harman suggested that the scheme could be extended to cover other offences such as death by dangerous driving.

The scheme is not without its critics. Circuit Judge John Samuels told a Radio 4 programme that allowing families to make statements might give them the impression they could influence the judge's sentence when that was not the case, adding that 'the use of statements raised the emotional temperature in courts and complicated judge's responsibilities'.

CRIMINAL INJURIES COMPENSATION SCHEME

The Criminal Injuries Compensation Authority administers the criminal injuries compensation scheme throughout Great Britain for those who have been the victim of a violent crime. Although the first scheme was set up in 1964, it was first revised in 1996 through the Criminal Injuries Compensation Act 1995, when the level of compensation was set by Parliament and according to a scale or tariff. This was further revised in 2001 and the tariff covers 25 levels of compensation, ranging from £1,000 to £250,000.

The scheme offers enhanced compensation for families of homicide victims.

A person is eligible to apply if, at the time of the deceased's death, they were:

(a) the partner of the deceased who is:

　　(i) a person who was living together with the deceased as husband and wife or as a same-sex partner in the same household immediately before the date of death and who, unless formally married to that person or a civil partner of that person, had been so living throughout the two years before the date; or

(ii) a spouse or civil partner or former spouse or civil partner of the deceased who was financially supported by him immediately before the date of death; or

(b) a natural parent of the deceased, or a person who was not the natural parent, provided that he was accepted by the deceased as a parent of his family; or

(c) a natural child of the deceased, or a person who was not the natural child, provided that he was accepted by the deceased as a child of his family or was dependent on him.

A person who was criminally responsible for the death of a victim may not be a qualifying claimant.

The standard compensation for each qualifying claimant in a fatal case is £5,500 (level 10 of the tariff) but, if there is only one qualifying claimant, this rises to £11,000 (level 13).

VICTIM SUPPORT
The charity organisation, Victim Support, has trained volunteers who can work with those dealing with bereavement following a homicide. When the police are involved in a case of murder or manslaughter, they should offer to put those people bereaved by the crime in touch with Victim Support. Direct contact may be made by the victim's friends and relatives. In addition to practical support, Victim Support publishes a leaflet, 'Murder and Manslaughter: Information for family and friends'.

VICTIM IMPACT AND VICTIM'S NEEDS
Though formal recognition of the rights and opinions of victims is clearly sound in principle, the cautious practitioner will recognise the delicate nature of the task and the potentially harmful effect of clumsy contact. Victim's needs are still not comprehensively understood and it is advisable to be wary of glib assumptions and shallow generalisations. Newburn (1993) provides an accessible if somewhat sweeping review of the literature and warns of the potentially severe and long-lasting emotional and psychological impact of violent crime upon direct and indirect victims, which can include: acute stage of grieving; persisting feelings of helplessness, anger, anxiety or depression; sleep disturbance; the recurrence of flashbacks; denial or suppression; social withdrawal or isolation; loss of concentration and impairment of memory; frequent change of address. Patterns of effect have been distilled into frameworks of understanding such as rape trauma syndrome (Burgess and Holmstrom, 1974) and homicide trauma syndrome (Burgess, 1975). More recently, post-traumatic stress disorder has been properly recognised as a consequence of serious crime (Kilpatrick et al, 1989).

Aubrey and Hossack (1994) are thus right to draw attention to the ethical and practical problems in putting Victims' Charter policy into effect and urge caution in approaching victims. For example:

'We cannot ensure that the initial letter will be opened by the addressee. Some individuals may have chosen to keep the crime event a secret; they may be in new families where the trauma has not been discussed. Alternatively, they may live alone and not have support to deal with the possible traumatic effect of reading the letter.'

There are no easy answers to such dilemmas and practice is still in its infancy. Johnston (1994) suggest that it is helpful to avoid posting an initial letter to arrive at the weekend when the recipient will be unable to telephone for clarification. Comfort can be drawn from research evidence that victims have an acute sense of the information gap between themselves and the criminal justice system. Brown *et al* (1990) noted that the families of murder victims wanted a greater say in the sentence planning process, feared that offenders might be released without their crime having been addressed and were particularly afraid of facing an unanticipated meeting with the offender on home leave or after release. In Johnston's small-scale research with nine victims' families who had experienced Victims' Charter enquiries in West Yorkshire (1994 and 1995), victims reported that contact with the Probation Service prior to the prisoner's release was essential to allay fears and to give a view in the pre-release planning process. Although anger was frequently expressed about the prospect of a prisoner's release, there was also a desire to give information about the impact of the release plan on themselves. Victims properly recognised that they did not have a deciding voice in whether the prisoner should be released or not, but were satisfied that they could influence the planning process.

'Some of those interviewed expressed concern about the impact of an approach by the Probation Service to the old or mentally unstable, especially if many years had elapsed between sentence and enquiry. On balance, however, it was felt by all those interviewed that it was preferable to know about the impending release, rather than have an unplanned chance encounter with the released prisoner. All felt that enquiries should be made even if the Probation Service had not established contact earlier in the sentence.'

In some enquiries, victims and families wished to know more about the offender, sometimes raising unanswered questions left over from the time of the offence and seeking communication directly or indirectly with the prisoner. Such requests have been assessed by West Yorkshire's specialist staff and the prisoner's home probation officer, and in some instances direct and indirect mediation work has proved possible and fruitful. Johnston (1994) gives a number of examples of this work, including the following:

> An elderly woman and her daughter, who had been victims of an arson attack on their home, asked to meet with the discretionary lifer responsible for the crime prior to his release which involved his return to live in their home area. Offender and victims had not known each other prior to the crime. They wished to hear his explanation of the offence and to make their own assessment of his expressions of remorse. The prisoner agreed and, with a mediator present, met them at their home during a period of temporary release for home leave. They accepted his apology and explanation and felt reassured and less anxious about his release.

> In the case of a mandatory lifer who had murdered an eight-year-old girl, a stranger to him, some 26 years previously, a step-daughter from the victim's family, now an adult but a child at the time of the killing, felt that she had grown up in the shadow of her deceased step-sister, to the extent that sometimes she was called by her step-sister's name by her step-father, the victim's father. She needed to put certain questions to the perpetrator to help her make sense of her childhood and move forward. She did not wish to meet the prisoner but was able to obtain his answers by indirect mediation.

Even if initiatives of this nature are either not sought or are not viable, the information gained from enquiries can enable more focused work on victim empathy to be undertaken with the lifer.

Probation staff contacting victim's families may find it instructive to note the comments of parents whose daughter had been murdered by her ex-fiancé and who were approached by the Service when the convicted man was being considered for release (Victim Support, Annual Report 1995):

> 'When the Probation Service contacted us to tell us about the parole we really felt that all they wanted to know was what I'd do to him if they let him out. They even talked about his family and said they had lost a son too! I asked if they could arrange home leave for (daughter) at the same time as arranging his.'

In 2006 Victim Support conducted a piece of research involving 41 people who had been bereaved by homicide. Their conclusions were published under the title, 'In the Aftermath – The Support Needs of People Bereaved by Homicide'. The research found, not surprisingly, that people experience bereavement by homicide in different ways depending on their relationship to the victim. Traumatic grief can be complicated by involvement in the criminal justice system, the processes of which can slow down grief reactions and intensify feelings of powerlessness and anger.

Key recommendations from the report, which are of interest to probation staff, include:

- a need for more active, practical help for bereaved families;
- a need to work closely with other organisations working with people bereaved by homicide;
- a need to review family liaison work;
- a need to improve communications and make sure that people can be helped more effectively;
- a need to update Victim Support training for volunteers working with bereaved people.

SAMM AND SELF-HELP

Relatives of homicide victims can obtain help from Support After Murder and Manslaughter (SAMM), a charity offering understanding and support to families and friends bereaved as a result of murder or manslaughter. Launched in 1994 as a development of the self-help group Parents of Murdered Children and based at Victim Support HQ, SAMM offers a national support network, encourages better understanding and sensitivity towards the impact of homicide, and supports research into the experience of victims' families. SAMM may be contacted at: Cranmer House, 39 Brixton Road, London SW9 6DZ, tel. 020 7735 3838 and http://www.samm.org.uk.

10
MENTALLY DISORDERED LIFERS

The status of lifers becomes more complex where they have been transferred to psychiatric hospital for treatment of their mental disorder under the transfer direction provisions of MHA 1983 s47 (invariably coupled with restrictions under s49) and are thus governed by both the 1983 Act and the 1991 Act. 'Mental disorder' means that the prisoner is suffering from mental illness, psychopathic disorder, mental impairment or severe mental impairment, the four forms of disorder regulated by the 1983 Act. The relevant mental health legislation, including the basis for a s47 direction, is detailed in Stone (1995, Chapters 13–14) but this Chapter seeks to clarify the mentally disordered lifer's particular predicament. Swinton *et al* (1994) report that between 1987 and 1990 an average of 25 lifers were transferred to hospital each year, and the number of lifers in psychiatric hospitals on 31 December each year varied between 161 and 165.

LIFE SENTENCE CLOCK
A prisoner's life sentence continues to run during any period of transfer and time spent in hospital counts towards the fulfilment of the lifer's tariff period.

REVIEW BY A MENTAL HEALTH REVIEW TRIBUNAL
Applications and Referrals
Lifers are in the same position as any determinate term prisoner subject to s47 provisions, together with a s49 restriction direction, and thus have the status of 'restricted patient'. A restriction direction is not automatic but is routinely added and will almost certainly be made where a lifer is concerned. They thus have the right to apply to a MHRT for a review of their patient status under MHA 1983 s70 at the following intervals:

(a) in the period between the expiration of six months and the expiration of 12 months, beginning with the date of the transfer direction; and

(b) in any subsequent period of 12 months.

In other words, after an initial application, the lifer can apply at yearly intervals. In the rare instance that a lifer is *not* subject to a s49 restriction direction, application to a MHRT may be made during the first six months of hospital detention from the date of their transfer direction and in any subsequent 12 month period: MHA 1983 s69(2).

In addition, the Home Secretary has a discretionary *power* under s71(1) to refer the lifer to a Tribunal *at any time*, and a *duty* to refer under s71(2) if their case has not been considered by a Tribunal within the last three years.

Notification to the Home Secretary
MHA 1983 s74(1)

Where an application to a Mental Health Review Tribunal is made by a restricted patient who is subject to a restriction direction, or where the case of such a patient is referred to such a tribunal, the tribunal:

(a) shall notify the Secretary of State whether, in their opinion, the patient would, if subject to a restriction order, be entitled to be absolutely or conditionally discharged (under MHA 1983 s73) above; and

(b) if they notify him that the patient would be entitled to be conditionally discharged, may recommend that in the event of his not being discharged under this section he should continue to be detained in hospital.

Following a hearing the Tribunal must notify the Home Secretary whether the lifer would be entitled, if s/he had been subject to a s37 hospital order coupled with a s41 restriction, to either an absolute or conditional discharge from hospital (s74(1)(a)). Such entitlement arises if the Tribunal is satisfied that one of the following criteria applies:

(i) the patient is not suffering from mental illness, psychopathic disorder, severe mental impairment or mental impairment; or

(ii) the patient is suffering from one of the four forms of disorder specified in (i) but not of a nature or degree which makes it appropriate for detention in hospital for medical treatment; or

(iii) it is not necessary for the health or safety of the patient or for the protection of other persons that s/he should receive such treatment.

If the Tribunal concludes that one of these criteria applies, the issue of whether discharge would, in the case of a s41 patient, be absolute or conditional depends on whether it is considered appropriate for the patient to remain liable to recall to hospital for further treatment. If conditional discharge (*ie* liability to recall) is considered to be appropriate, the Tribunal may recommend that the patient should remain in hospital rather than be returned to prison (s74(1)(b)).

Even if the Tribunal does not consider that one of the criteria (i)–(iii) applies, it nevertheless has the discretion to notify the Home Secretary that the lifer no longer requires treatment or that no effective treatment can be given.

112

HOME SECRETARY'S POWERS

The Secretary of State has three sets of statutory powers in respect of the lifer patient.

(i) Following a MHRT review, as detailed above, the provisions of s74(2) may apply:

MHA 1983 s74

(2) If in the case of a patient ...

    (a) the tribunal notify the Secretary of State that the patient would be entitled to be absolutely or conditionally discharged; and

    (b) within the period of 90 days beginning with the date of that notification the Secretary of State gives notice to the tribunal that the patient may be so discharged,

the tribunal shall direct the absolute or, as the case may be, the conditional discharge of the patient.

(3) Where a patient continues to be liable to be detained in a hospital at the end of the period referred to in subsection (2)(b) above because the Secretary of State has not given the notice there mentioned, the managers of the hospital shall, unless the tribunal have made a recommendation under subsection (1)(b) above, transfer the patient to a prison or other institution in which he might have been detained if he had not been removed to hospital, there to be dealt with as if he had not been so removed.

    ....

(5) Where a patient is transferred or remitted under subsection (3) ... above the relevant transfer direction and the restriction direction shall cease to have effect on his arrival in the prison or other institution.

(ii) At any time, s42(2) gives the Minister power of absolute or conditional discharge:

MHA 1983 s42(2)

At any time while a restriction order is in force in respect of a patient, the Secretary of State may, if he thinks fit, by warrant discharge the patient from hospital, either absolutely or subject to conditions; and where a person is absolutely discharged under this subsection, he shall thereupon cease to be liable to be detained by virtue of the relevant hospital order, and the restriction order shall cease to have effect accordingly.

(iii) Upon notification that treatment is no longer necessary or effective, the discretionary provisions of s50(1) may arise:

MHA 1983 s50

(1) Where a transfer direction and a restriction direction have been given in respect of a person serving a sentence of imprisonment and before the expiration of that person's sentence the Secretary of State is notified by the responsible medical officer, any other registered medical practitioner or a Mental Health Review Tribunal that that person no longer requires treatment in hospital for mental disorder or that no effective treatment for his disorder can be given in the hospital to which he has been removed, the Secretary of State may –

   (a) by warrant direct that he be remitted to any prison or other institution in which he might have been detained if he had not been removed to hospital, there to be dealt with as if he had not been so removed; or

   (b) exercise any power of releasing him on licence or discharging him under supervision which would have been exercisable if he had been remitted to such a prison or institution as aforesaid,

   and on his arrival in the prison or other institution or, as the case may be, his release or discharge as aforesaid, the transfer direction and the restriction direction shall cease to have effect.

(2) A restriction direction in the case of a person serving a sentence of imprisonment shall cease to have effect upon the expiration of the sentence.

Put another way, the Secretary of State has the following options:

(i)   discharge into the community under s42(2) or s74; or

(ii) release on licence under s50(1)(b); or

(iii) return to prison under s50(1)(a), thus terminating the transfer direction.

Under previous policy, it was the normal practice to release lifers under s42(2) on a warrant of conditional discharge (rather than under the provisions of s74) but in a Parliamentary written answer of 23 July 1985, the Home Secretary announced that in future s50(1)(b) would usually be applied instead, *ie* release on life licence on the recommendation of the Parole Board and after consultation with the judiciary but without the necessity to return to prison prior to release, provided that the tariff date has passed.

The policy statement indicated that discharge under s42(2) would be more appropriate only in 'exceptional circumstances', where the Lord Chief Justice (and the trial judge, if available) so recommend. The Report of the Parole Board for 1985 (para. 18) indicated:

'In the main, such cases will be where the Court would have made a hospital order under MHA 1983 but was constrained from doing so by the unavailability of a hospital bed.'

This exceptional course would also seem appropriate for offenders who are subsequently found to have been suffering a mental disorder at the time of their offence but this was not apparent at the time of sentence.

Such lifers are termed 'technical lifers', defined by the Court of Appeal in *R v Secretary of State, ex parte H* [1995] QB 43 as 'those who committed offences when mentally disordered, in relation to whom for some reason a hospital order was not made by the sentencing judge'.

A 'technical' life sentence will thus only arise in discretionary life cases. The Court of Appeal, in considering the case of such a lifer sentenced before the 1991 Act, indicated that 'punishment of such a person being inappropriate, the tariff is incapable of certification under CJA 1991 Sch 12 para. 9'. The Court did not indicate how the trial judge would now deal with such a case under the provisions of s34.

The intention of the 1985 policy was thus that most s47 lifers would first be subject to review under mental health provisions, with subsequent referral to the Parole Board in appropriate cases. The policy sought to ensure that the principle of the life sentence (that it should be life long) should not be undermined and to promote consistency of treatment among lifers. In *R v Secretary of State, ex parte S* (1992) *The Times*, 19 August, a s47 lifer sought to challenge the policy arguing that it deprived those affected of the potential benefit of absolute discharge without liability to supervision or recall and that the Home Secretary had unlawfully fettered his discretion. This was rejected by Henry J who determined that the policy was a legitimate and rational exercise of ministerial discretion promoting consistency and predictability, while leaving it open to a lifer to make representations to be dealt with other than by s50 procedures which would then be considered on the merits of the individual case.

Following implementation of the 1991 Act, however, in the case of *ex parte H* (above) four prisoner-patients who had received discretionary life sentences sought to argue that the 1991 Act provisions now take precedence and that they should be able to pursue a DLP hearing despite their continuing s47 status. Though initially successful before the Divisional Court ([1994] QB 378), their claim was denied on the Home Secretary's appeal to the Court of Appeal which concluded that the right to a DLP hearing, either under s34(5) for those sentenced since the 1991 Act or under Sch 12 para. 9 for pre-dating discretionary lifers, was not conferred on s47 patients, given that they have a right to a periodic Tribunal hearing which has judicial characteristics akin to a DLP.

Of the four lifers, two were 'technical lifers' and could thus expect to be discharged under s42(2), while one other who too was still receiving treatment was required to await the outcome of a Tribunal hearing. The fourth man had already been reviewed by a Tribunal that had notified the Home Office under s74(1) that if he were subject to a restriction order he would be entitled to be conditionally discharged but, if not discharged, he should remain in hospital rather than be returned to prison, as this might cause a relapse in his mental condition. Because he did not require further treatment, he alone was entitled to be referred to the Parole Board for a DLP hearing, albeit that he remained in hospital. In a written Parliamentary answer on 20 June 1994 the Secretary of State had already confirmed that discretionary lifers whom it is not appropriate to return to prison but who no longer require, or can effectively be given, treatment are referred to the Parole Board in exactly the same way as if they had been remitted to prison.

As part of the same case, the Court of Appeal also dismissed a similar claim by Michael Hickey, a lifer initially sentenced at age 17 to HMP detention for murder, who argued that, having served the tariff part of his sentence, he could now require the Secretary of State to refer his case to the Parole Board under CJA 1991 s35. The Court noted that he was shortly to be assessed by a MHRT and that there was:

> 'nothing improper or irrational in the Secretary of State awaiting the outcome of the Tribunal hearing ... Thereafter, it may become appropriate for Mr Hickey either to be released under s50(1)(b) or for him to be returned to prison where he can have the benefit of s35(2).'

(per Rose LJ)

The Home Office had accepted that the Parliamentary answer of 20 June 1994 applies equally to mandatory lifers who can thus be reviewed by the Board even though remaining in hospital.

Review Following Return to Prison

Where a lifer has been returned (or 'remitted') to prison from hospital under s50(1)(a), their process of review will depend upon the extent of their completion of their tariff period. Their first or subsequent review date may have passed during their time in hospital. *LM* para. 15.7 identifies the following process:

(i) Where the first review date (*ie* at three years before expiry of the tariff) is at least one year ahead, the date will be set in the usual way.

(ii) If the first review date is less than 12 months after the date of remission and the prisoner had not been notified of the first review date before being transferred to hospital, the review date will be one year from the date of remission.

116

(iii) If the prisoner had been notified of the first review date, the review will be held on that date unless the prisoner is prepared to agree that it is in his or her interest to set a later review date so that proper assessments may be made. If so the prisoner must be asked formally to request a later date.

(iv) If the first or subsequent review date has passed without a review, or where the prisoner has been formally reviewed before the time of transfer to hospital, the review date will be one year after remission to prison, unless there are strong reasons to consider an earlier review date.

(v) In the case of discretionary lifers who have served their tariff, the case will generally be referred to the Parole Board as soon as they return to prison. The Parole Board will decide the date of the Discretionary Lifer Panel Hearing. The referral of the case may be delayed if the prisoner makes a formal request to that effect.

It will thus be apparent that the process of review will often be slowed down because of the period of transfer. According to 'Justice' (1996), the Home Office currently requires discretionary lifers returned to prison from hospital to wait a further year in prison conditions before their DLP hearing.

RECENT PAROLE BOARD REVIEWS

Of 20 cases of 'hospital transferees' considered by the Board in 1993–94, eight were recommended for release on licence, three out of eleven in 1993 and five out of nine in 1994 (*Parole Board Annual Report*, 1994).

Licence Condition

'Where release is recommended, it will be subject to inclusion in the life licence of medical oversight as well as the usual conditions of supervision by the Probation Service' (*Parole Board Annual Report*, 1985).

ROLE OF THE PROBATION SERVICE

Transferred lifers will be subject to post-release supervision by the Probation Service, whether conditionally discharged or released on life licence, and thus pre-release/discharge contact will be appropriate in the normal way, in accordance with National Standards.

DANGEROUS AND SEVERE PERSONALITY DISORDER

Following on from a manifesto commitment of the New Labour Government when it came into power in 1997, four 'Dangerous and Severe Personality Disorder' projects were set up in two prisons and two high security hospitals in England. Over 300 places have been made available at:

- HMP Frankland – Westgate Unit (80 places)
- HMP Whitemoor – Ferns Unit D Wing (84 places)
- Broadmoor – The Paddocks Centre (70 places)
- Rampton; Peaks Unit (70 places)

While the majority of prisoners likely to meet the DSPD criteria are men, there is a group of women within the prison estate – between 10 and 15 in number – who are thought likely to benefit from intervention and placed at the Primrose Project at HMP Low Newton, Durham. While some determinate sentence prisoners are also beneficiaries of the projects, there is a high proportion of life sentence prisoners within the schemes. Of the first intake of 55 men onto the Whitemoor project, 76% were serving life sentences and 38% of these were for murder (Taylor, 2003).

The projects are aimed at supporting public protection through the development of pilot treatment services for dangerous offenders whose offending is linked to Dangerous and Severe Personality Disorder. Admissions to DSPD hospital units must satisfy the requirements of the Mental Health Act 1983 and referral criteria and referral forms can be found in Probation Circular 40/2006 – *Dangerous and Severe Personality Disorder (DSPD) Programme.*

DSPD is not without its critics. The need to 'do something' about untreatable personality disorders was undoubtedly caused by the reaction to the murders of Lin and Megan Russell in 1996. A Home Affairs select committee report summed up the ensuing dilemma thus:

> 'The murders committed by Michael Stone caused very real alarm and raised very difficult questions as to the reconciliation of two powerful forces – the need to protect the civil liberties of those who have not committed an offence and the need to protect society from the offence the may commit.'

(Third Special Report, 1999)

DSPD has no legal or medical basis and so it is perhaps no surprise that some doctors regard it as a political invention brought about by the events described above with serious implications for civil liberties. This was outlined in the Lancet, suggesting that six people would have to be detained to prevent one from acting violently (*The Guardian,* 17 April 2002).

11
CASE ILLUSTRATIONS

A MANDATORY LIFE SENTENCE
Though this case arises from HMP detention under CYPA 1933 s53(1) and should now be regarded as akin to a discretionary life sentence (see pages 110–12), it nevertheless illustrates the mandatory life process under procedures to date. This account is drawn from files held by the current home area probation officer and thus does not necessarily reflect the full range of opinions or events which have shaped the assessment of this case. It nevertheless presents a substantial flavour of the pace, concerns, roles and responsibilities in the course of a mandatory lifer's progress from sentence to the point where their release is within sight.

Michael Howerd

Offence
Murder by shooting of a boy aged 12, a distant relative, whom Michael Howerd, aged 15 at the time of the offence and sentence, suspected of stealing from the Howerd family. The prosecution evidence suggested that the killing and disposal of the body had been planned and pursued with an unusual degree of cool calculation. Michael Howerd had no previous convictions.

Trial Judge's Opinion to Home Secretary
Michael Howerd must be regarded as a very dangerous youth who had shown callous disregard for human life and should be incarcerated 'for a very long time indeed' – 'were he an adult, I would have recommended that he be not released for about 12 years. I appreciate that at his comparatively young age some marked change in his personality may yet occur which would justify a somewhat shorter period'.

First Phase of Sentence
Located initially on the 'young prisoner' wings of two large local prisons, he is transferred at age 18 to a youth custody centre. Notified there that his first Parole Board Review will take place 12 years after sentence (*ie* implying a tariff period of 15 years), he is clearly disappointed by such a distant target date but is said to have 'coped philosophically'. Life Sentence Review Boards note his conforming behaviour and his good use of time but are concerned at his quiet, self-contained manner and reluctance to discuss his offence, interpreted as cold, controlled, defensive detachment so that his 'true self' remains unknown. Medical reports speculate about Mr Howerd's latent psychiatric disturbance

and aggression. It is thus felt important that his next location should have a 'psychiatric resource' so that his personality can be examined in depth.

Second Phase of Sentence

At age 21 Mr Howerd is re-allocated to an adult Cat. B prison where his 'inner turmoil' is further speculated about but not made subject of sustained psychiatric attention. Transferred on to a further Cat. B prison at age 24, he is still considered to be a 'largely unknown quantity' and his self-control and apparent contentment continue to be viewed suspiciously. He is now heavily committed to art classes and painting in his personal time. Though this is considered a productive use of time, staff become concerned with the 'distorted and disturbing' subject matter of some of his work and it is considered that this merits investigation by a psychologist skilled in art interpretation to see if any mental disturbance might be indicated. This suggestion prompts a spirited response from the prison art teacher who points out that she had set the group an exercise specifically to explore the depiction of distorted images and that the paintings validly reflect the sadness, isolation and despair of prison life.

Staff continue to articulate worries prompted by Mr Howerd's evenness of mood and wonder why 'he never gets wound up about anything' – a wing officer believes that 'the real Michael Howerd is waiting to erupt' and a chaplain expresses a 'gut feeling that he presents an extremely high risk to others' because he has not demonstrated compassion or remorse in his discussions of his offence. A prison-based probation officer seeks to counter the common perception of Mr Howerd's 'detached and emotionless' personality by identifying his upbringing in a family inhibited in communication and the expression of emotion, making his self-containment hardly surprising. His lack of affect could thus be viewed as a self-disciplined coping mechanism. In the meantime, Mr Howerd has formed a relationship with a woman living away from his home area and is planning to live with her and attend Art College on his release. She is 16 years older than him.

Transfer to Cat. C

On Mr Howerd's transfer to less secure conditions at age 27, reports to the LSRB are favourable, suggesting that first impressions of a cold, unfeeling person are misleading and that, with patience and understanding, he reveals a creative, thoughtful personality. A better understanding begins to emerge of the 15-year-old Michael Howerd who had experienced his father's apparent lack of interest and considerable anxiety about his mother's psychiatric problems and her associated attempted suicide. He had appeared to believe that if he could 'get rid' of the boy who he believed to be causing particular pressure on family life, he would help to erase his family's problems. He now seems genuinely remorseful for the waste of two young lives. In the light of favourable reports, progress achieved and acceptance that earlier reports had misjudged Mr Howerd's character, an escorted 'day out' (or, more formally, a 'familiarisation visit') is arranged to a local town which goes well. As Mr Howerd's art has attracted positive attention from the Chief Inspector of Prisons, it is felt in his best interests to return to his previous Cat. B prison, not for security reasons but because it offers better art education facilities so that he will be better placed to seek entry into a polytechnic foundation course. This transfer proves unfruitful because the course is no longer available and Mr Howerd returns to Cat. C.

First Parole Board Review (age 29)

In the light of the Board's recommendation, the Home Secretary decides that Mr Howerd should be transferred to open conditions, with a further review in two years.

Open Prison Phase

(i)   Approved for escorted visits after eight weeks, Mr Howerd is taken to visit his proposed partner at her home. Shortly afterwards he informs his original home area probation officer (who remains responsible for throughcare) that he no longer wishes to continue the relationship or to pursue that release plan and indicates that he has been corresponding with another woman and that this relationship has now intensified, though they have not yet met. He now seeks an escorted visit to her home with a view to unescorted home leave. She lives with her son aged 14. A probation officer in her home area interviews her and also notifies Social Services of this proposal given Mr Howerd's status as a Sch 1 offender, under *CI 45/78* 'child at risk' procedures. The planned transfer of throughcare responsibility to the original proposed partner's Probation Area is cancelled.

(ii)   Approved for unescorted journeys following six months satisfactory behaviour in open conditions (under the pre-April 1995 procedures), Mr Howerd commences a course at a nearby college of further education, two days a week.

(iii) While awaiting Social Service's decision, Mr Howerd is escorted first to a Koestler art exhibition featuring one of his works and then on a successful day visit to his new proposed partner's home.

(iv)   Seven months after receiving notification, Social Services convene a Child Protection Case Conference, attended by the open prison's Lifer Governor and seconded probation officer, the probation officer from Mr Howerd's original home area and the senior probation officer for the new partner's area. Her son is entered on the Child Protection Register in the category of 'likely physical abuse', a keyworker from Social Services is identified and a package of support and monitoring of home leave is agreed, with a further review in six months.

(v) First unescorted home leave is agreed and proves successful, though Mr Howerd overlooks his requirement to report to the local probation office, an oversight resolved by a prompt home visit. A second satisfactory home leave follows. A LSRB meeting indicates that Mr Howerd can expect release at age 33, when his partner's son will be 18 and no longer subject to child protection procedures. Throughcare responsibility is formally transferred to a probation officer in his partner's home area.

(vi) Following the introduction of Temporary Licence (see Chapter 6), a fresh Risk Assessment has to be completed before Mr Howerd is able to take further home leave (or Resettlement Licence, as now renamed) or continue his college attendance (now Facility Licence). The home probation officer re-assesses the home circumstances and indicates that further home leave presents no cause for anxiety. The boy relates well to Mr Howerd though it is impossible to predict how he would react if Mr Howerd were to join the household permanently. He remains on the Child Protection Register.

(vii) Anticipating the next Parole Board Review and the preliminary interview with a Board member, the LSRB informs Mr Howerd that 'he must have some ideas about why he should be released and his plans for the future', as well as showing that 'he has changed since his offence and that he felt remorse'. He is invited to rehearse what he wants to say with relevant LSRB members.

(viii) To fulfil Victims Charter responsibilities, the proposed resettlement area probation officer contacts relatives of the murdered boy and receives letters urging the Parole Board to recommend against release, because the time served to date by Mr Howerd does not adequately reflect the crime – the family still consider Mr Howerd to be dangerous and it would cause anguish if he returned to visit his family who remain living in the same small community as the victim's relatives. They have contacted their local MP who has also expressed concern about the impact that Mr Howerd's release could have in that area. In his report to the Parole Board, prepared eight months before its second review, the home area probation officer suggests a licence requirement that Mr Howerd should not visit his parents at their home. Release via a PRES hostel is recommended.

(ix) Following concern expressed by Social Services that their workers have not been reliably notified of Mr Howerd's periods of Resettlement Licence with his partner and some uncertainty about where the burden of responsibility lies for informing that agency, it is agreed that the home area probation officer will pass on this information. A further five-day leave is agreed, towards the end of which the partner's son informs his social worker that Mr Howerd and his mother have 'had a bust up'. Mr Howerd has not mentioned any problem when reporting to the probation office but his partner subsequently confirms that the relationship has encountered difficulties and is now over. Shortly after his return to the prison, Mr Howerd writes to his probation officer that the relationship has ended by mutual agreement, suggesting that this is partly because of the pressures created by Social Services' monitoring procedures. He indicates that he will not seek further periods of Resettlement Licence to that address and requests help in establishing a new release plan.

(x)   The home area probation officer embarks on a new initiative seeking the help of the probation housing team in a city known slightly to Mr Howerd where he now feels he would like to settle on release. The officer's addendum report to the Parole Board sketches these tentative new proposals. The Parole Board considers the case (Mr Howerd is now aged 31 and has served approximately 15 years) and defers further consideration, requiring a fuller report about the relationship breakdown and the revised release plan.

(xi) Following the initially somewhat reluctant agreement of the probation team in the proposed resettlement area to accept transfer of responsibility, two escorted visits to that city so that Mr Howerd can orientate himself and meet staff there, and further reports as requested, the Parole Board recommends his release.

(xii) The Home Secretary authorises Mr Howerd's release, subject to a satisfactory completion of a period in a PRES hostel close to the proposed resettlement area. He is given a provisional release date which would mean his release on licence 16 years after sentence.

A DISCRETIONARY LIFE SENTENCE
Leo Brittan

Offence

Leo Brittan's offence was wounding with intent to murder. Seeking to obtain details of his wife's whereabouts from her brother who refused to disclose any information, Mr Brittan threatened to kill him with a firearm. The victim was shot four times. Mr Brittan denied any intention to kill his brother-in-law, claiming that he had merely wanted to frighten him, but was convicted after trial. Mr Brittan had numerous previous convictions for dishonesty but none for violence.

Sentence (age 36)

In the light of medical evidence of emotional instability and psychopathic personality, life imprisonment plus concurrent determinate terms of seven and four years for related offences (sentence was imposed shortly before the Hodgson guideline case – see page 26). In a subsequent letter to the Home Secretary, the trial judge considered it likely that Mr Brittan ('probably an aggressive psychopath') 'will be a danger to the public for many years'.

Experience Prior to the Criminal Justice Act 1991

First Parole Board Review (after 10½ years)

This recommended a further review in two years.

Second Parole Board Review (after 13 years)

This was initially deferred pending a fresh psychiatric report which indicated no mental health problems or indications of psychopathy. The Board subsequently recommended transfer to open prison and a further review after 12 months. Mr Brittan was instead transferred to another closed prison.

Third Parole Board Review (after 14½ years)

Considered suitable for release by the LRC, the Board recommended release subject to 18 months in open prison and six months in a PRES hostel. Mr Brittan was accordingly transferred to Cat. D prison and to PRES a year later.

PRES Hostel (after 16 years)

Following an incident when he allegedly threatened youths with a kitchen knife because they had insulted him, he was charged with ABH and carrying an offensive weapon and remanded to a local prison. Eventually acquitted, he expected to resume his route to release but was transferred immediately back to a dispersal prison. The Home Secretary had received reports of other aggressive behaviour while Mr Brittan was at the PRES hostel, in particular that he had been barred from a Job Centre after intimidating staff. A further medical report had assessed him as 'paranoid and deteriorating'.

Fourth Parole Board Review (after 17½ years)

This review considered that Mr Brittan continued to pose 'enormous risk' and recommended further review after three years.

Fifth Parole Board Review (after 21 years)

This considered Mr Brittan unsuitable for release and recommended further review after three years.

After the Criminal Justice Act 1991

Tariff

The Home Secretary certified Mr Brittan's penal term as 15 years (Sch 12, para. 9).

First Discretionary Lifer Panel Hearing

The hearing that was initially scheduled to take place 25½ years after sentence was deferred for seven months at the request of Mr Brittan's solicitor, who wished to secure a fresh psychiatric assessment. Ultimately, Mr Brittan opted not to instruct his solicitor further and declined to co-operate in any formal assessment of his suitability for release or to appear in person before the Panel. The Medical Officer of the dispersal prison in which Mr Brittan was then housed expressed concern about his abnormal mental state and suggested that he might be suffering a paranoid psychotic illness. Not surprisingly, the Panel felt unable to order his release, citing Mr Brittan's refusal to address his offending behaviour or to co-operate with assessment, and also made no recommendation with regard to transfer, simply stating an expectation that an up-to-date psychiatric report would be provided for the next DLP review.

Subsequent Transfers

Three months after the DLP Mr Brittan was transferred to a Cat. C prison but within six months was transferred on to a Cat. B establishment following an incident in which he had broken a window in his cell because he considered the ventilation inadequate.

Lifer Review Board (after 27 years)

Taking a more sympathetic view of Mr Brittan's outlook, the Board noted that he had presented no problems in the period of five months at the Cat. B prison but identified his 'independent spirit' and somewhat eccentric and entrenched viewpoint. The Board recognised that he must despair at times of ever being released and be doubtful of ever satisfying 'the system'. Though his history in Cat. C confinement was unpromising, the Board considered that he deserved perseverance and support and suggested early transfer to a fresh Cat. C establishment, backed by a willingness to receive him back at his present prison if such a transfer proved unsuccessful.

Subsequent Transfers

Following the LRB's suggestion, Mr Brittan was transferred to a Cat. C prison but this proved an unhappy experience both for the prisoner and staff and six months later, after a further confrontational incident and a few weeks before his next scheduled DLP hearing, he was transferred back to a dispersal prison. Aggrieved at this transfer and in dispute with staff about personal property to which he was denied access, Mr Brittan was verbally confrontational to staff and received a penalty of 14 days segregation. He subsequently opted to remain in the segregation unit because he was not able to return to the wing of his choice.

During his most recent period at a Cat. C prison, one of Mr Brittan's friends who was concerned at his lengthy incarceration wrote to a prominent penal reformer, a member of the House of Lords, seeking to interest him in taking up his case. This peer in turn contacted Mr Brittan's outside probation officer in the area in which he hoped eventually to settle, seeking further details of Mr Brittan's case, and in the light of this information, wrote to the Home Secretary, receiving a reply from a junior minister. Subsequently, Lifer Group staff wrote to the probation officer's Chief Officer expressing disquiet that the officer appeared to have tried inappropriately to exert pressure through the peer to gain Mr Brittan's transfer to an open prison. The CPO replied that the officer had acted properly and professionally and no criticism was justified.

Anticipating the Second DLP (after 28 years)

Shortly before the scheduled DLP hearing at the Cat. C prison and after Mr Brittan's transfer back to a dispersal prison, the Home Office contacted his solicitor suggesting that the hearing should be adjourned. Reports had not been prepared at the Cat. C establishment prior to his relocation. The solicitor expressed puzzlement as to why reports had not been completed in time and declined consent to an adjournment, suggesting that this would seem appropriate only if Mr Brittan could be transferred back to the Cat. C prison and 'given a clear run there' before a panel hearing in approximately three months time. In the meantime, a fresh psychiatric report had been obtained on Mr Brittan's behalf which identified that he had acquired an entrenched reputation as a truculent, arrogant, litigious, paranoid prisoner which had followed him around the prison system over many years. The psychiatrist agreed that Mr Brittan expressed a rigidity of view which had caused him to engage in frequent and futile anti-establishment battles, but nevertheless found no evidence of mental disorder or of any physical violence apart from the index offence. The report noted also his practical intelligence, artistic interests and constructive abilities.

Reports to the Panel

Reports by prison staff referred to Mr Brittan remaining 'as obnoxious and obstructive as ever', and to his seemingly bleak future of institutionalised old age – 'his inability to be perceived as rational makes his release almost certainly impossible'. His confrontational behaviour was considered to 'raise concern that physical violence might occur'. In the light of these assessments, the Secretary of State's view was that Mr Brittan was not suitable for release and 'he should remain in closed conditions to address his offending behaviour and in particular his behaviour which leads him to be verbally aggressive towards staff'. The home area probation officer fully accepted that Mr Brittan was difficult and uncompromising, making him verbally aggressive and unco-operative towards staff but suggested that this was his way of asserting his independence and his refusal to accept that his crime warranted a life sentence. The officer queried whether the facts demonstrated Mr Brittan's continuing danger to the public. The officer had been responsible for Mr Brittan's throughcare for five years since he had decided that his residual ties with his original home area were no longer tenable and had opted to plan his resettlement in a fresh area. Having been on the waiting list for a Housing Association flat throughout that period, Mr Brittan would now be offered a tenancy, subject to a short preliminary period of assessment at a local probation hostel. He had already formed links with a church community in that area as well as with other interested individuals and volunteers.

The Hearing

Sitting at the Cat. C prison from which Mr Brittan had been transferred and to which he was brought specifically from the dispersal prison's segregation unit, the Panel, chaired by a High Court judge, deliberated for nearly five hours, hearing evidence from Mr Brittan, from the home area probation officer, a prison chaplain, a senior member of Mr Brittan's religious organisation and two members of the community who had known Mr Brittan over several years, and from a prison governor and principal prison officer for the Secretary of State.

The Decision

The Panel ultimately ordered Mr Brittan's release on licence 'within fifteen days' of its written decision, adding two additional licence conditions:

(i) Residing initially at the probation hostel and thereafter at the Housing Association flat;

(ii) compliance 'with any requirements reasonably imposed by your supervising officer for the purpose of ensuring that you continue to address your offending behaviour problems'.

In reaching their decision, the Panel specifically identified the following reasons:

(i) the absence of any convictions for violence prior to or since the offence;

(ii) although Mr Brittan's behaviour has been perceived as obsessive and intimidating, 'there is no specific allegation of violence on your part in the recent past';

(iii) though Mr Brittan had 'not worked on the nature of your offence and the effects on your victim, since it is now 28 years on, the Panel did not regard that as crucial to their decision';

(iv) the view of the home area probation officer that, in his mid-sixties, the sooner Mr Brittan was taken out of the prison system, the better his prospect of rehabilitation;

127

(v) the excellent and carefully thought-out release plan put forward by the home area probation officer, addressing Mr Brittan's needs, coupled with the presence of a number of supportive friends.

Release

Released from the Cat. C prison rather than being returned to disposal prison, Mr Brittan was met at the gate by his probation officer. The prison was unable to offer space or opportunity to sort through and rationalise his accumulated property prior to release and they were obliged to do this in the probation officer's car in woodland nearby, a regrettable final note on which to leave the prison system.

Comment

Though this lifer had clearly served an untypically protracted period of custody extending 13 years beyond tariff expiry and including time at 54 prisons, his case was not specially selected for that reason but rather to illustrate how the essential issue of dangerousness and risk facing a DLP needs to be distinguished from other features of the lifer's prison behaviour. Mr Brittan had consistently refused to 'play the game' throughout the turbulent course of his prison career. In the words of one report, he was reluctant to accept what he perceived as 'hoops to be jumped through to satisfy a system which he now despises and which seems not particularly well disposed towards him'. Though he had done himself few favours, his stance seems partly the product of the less purposeful and perceptive lifer system of old, but the system of the present day continued to find him a frustrating irritant and assumed that he was stuck indefinitely in the closed prison carousel. His record of awkwardness, stubbornness and verbal confrontation, coupled with somewhat unsubstantiated or hearsay fears that his aggression could escalate to physical violence, proved insufficient evidence to justify his continued detention, especially given a clear and constructive release plan that would allow him private space and opportunity to pursue his own priorities and lifestyle.

A DISCRETIONARY LIFER PANEL HEARING
The Prisoner
Douglas Herd, aged 38.

The Offence
Convicted at age 22 of manslaughter of a woman in the course of a robbery.

Previous DLP Hearings and Subsequent Events
Mr Herd's first DLP, shortly after the introduction of this review procedure and some 32 months before the hearing described, had recommended

his transfer to Cat. D conditions and the Secretary of State adopted this recommendation, transferring him to an open prison. After 12 months and following the commencement of home leave opportunities, he absconded as a response to stress. He surrendered himself shortly afterwards and was located in a local prison for five months before transfer to his current Cat. C prison. After acknowledging a substantial sexual dimension to his index offence, he was moved to a vulnerable prisoners unit (VPU) which offered the core sex offender treatment programme (SOTP) which he opted not to undertake. At his next DLP, 26 months after his first panel and six months before the hearing described below, he asked to be transferred back to Cat. D conditions but the panel indicated that he should be given a further opportunity to undertake SOTP and that the hearing would reconvene in six months time. The hearing now described is the reconvened panel sitting.

The Hearing

Commencement
The parties, witnesses and observers (in this instance, the prison parole clerk and the author) waited outside until called into the room by the member of the Parole Board Secretariat acting as Panel Secretary.

Seating
All participants remained seated at a table throughout, following a standard Parole Board seating plan, as illustrated:

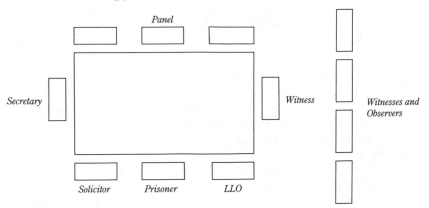

Introduction
(i) The Chairman introduced the Panel, the participants and the observers and indicated at the outset that the reports to the Panel all indicated that Mr Herd should be transferred to open prison and that this was now the recommendation of the Home Secretary.

129

(ii) The Lifer Liaison Officer, given the opportunity to comment on the recommendation, had nothing to add.

(iii) Mr Herd's solicitor indicated that Mr Herd was seeking his immediate release either to a hostel or to accommodation secured by the Probation Service or placement at a PRES hostel, but otherwise would support transfer to a Cat. D establishment.

(iv) The solicitor was given the opportunity to ask the LLO any questions but had none.

Prisoner's Evidence

(i) Questions from his solicitor covered his experience of the SOTP; his previous experience at an open prison; the reasons why he had absconded and his subsequent early surrender to custody; his reluctance to return to open prison (possibility of recognition and assault as an ex-Rule 43 sexual offender, the likely unavailability there of further prison courses from which he could benefit, the limited scope for temporary release opportunities, the greater opportunity to gain support and counselling if freed or located in a PRES hostel).

(ii) Panel members' questions addressed: why the risk of assault would be reduced in a PRES hostel; his previous reliance on prescribed medication and cannabis; the factors which had been shown to cause him stress and how he would cope if he experienced these together; his difficulties in coping with dormitory living in previous establishments; how the SOTP course had changed his outlook and whether he had been able to apply the knowledge gained; what further work he felt he needed to achieve on 'relationships' and whether an open prison might provide this opportunity.

(iii) Given the opportunity to question Mr Herd and comment on his evidence, the LLO acknowledged his progress, suggested that the prisoner was now better equipped to cope with the demands of Cat. D (Mr Herd agreed) and asked if he was aware of one open prison in particular which provided single accommodation and housed a large number of sex offender lifers. In what proved to be the most adversarial moment of the Hearing, the LLO next questioned Mr Herd about a recent incident at the prison, for which he had been punished on Governor's Adjudication, when he had refused to go from the VPU where he was accommodated to the prison hospital to provide a sample for a routine drug testing procedure. Clearly unhappy that this had been raised, Mr Herd sought to justify his refusal, claiming that on a previous occasion when he had been taken to the hospital he had been left unattended in the company of other prisoners from the main part of the prison and at risk of assault. The LLO indicated that on the subsequent occasion he had received a Governor's guarantee of his safety. This led the chairman to comment on his apparent intransigence and his need to accept a code of rules in life, even if they can feel unpalatable. Would he be able to live by hostel rules, for example? Mr Herd indicated that he did not see that as a comparable situation.

(iv) Mr Herd's solicitor opted not to question him further in re-examination but asked the LLO to clarify the issue of transfer to a Cat. D prison with individual accommodation. The LLO indicated that only three open establishments currently received sex offenders and he would seek to ensure that Mr Herd was allocated to the establishment already mentioned which he regarded as the most appropriate.

First Witness (Prison Psychologist)

(i) Though called by the prisoner and able to speak of Mr Herd's progress, the psychologist indicated in reply to the prisoner's solicitor that he supported transfer to Cat. D conditions, as the 'ideal test situation' which could provide a valuable learning experience, despite Mr Herd's genuine fears and doubts. While agreeing that a hostel could provide greater support, the witness considered that an open prison could provide necessary experience for Mr Herd in tackling demands and pressures for himself and that this would enhance his confidence. Asked about the scope for further beneficial courses available to Mr Herd in an open prison, the witness suggested that a 'booster' or refresher SOTP course (see page 41) would be both available and beneficial. Mr Herd was asked by his solicitor if there was anything further he wished to be taken up with the witness, but he declined.

(ii) Panel members clarified with the witness the nature of a SOTP 'booster' programme and whether this would be available in the community if Mr Herd was released immediately. They also asked him to expand on part of his written report referring to Mr Herd's 'avoidance' in thinking through his original offence behaviour and future situations which might present 'an echo' of the original offence.

(iii) The LLO opted not to question the witness and Mr Herd's solicitor had no further questions.

Second Witness (Prison Probation Officer responsible for SOTP)

(i) In response to the solicitor, the witness clarified his SOTP role and when asked to give a view on release *versus* Cat. D, supported the latter, considering that otherwise Mr Herd would 'miss out a stage' and that there would be more probation expertise available at an open prison than at a hostel. The witness was then asked what particular probation work he considered Mr Herd needed in Cat. D conditions and what would be the role of the home area probation officer during the Cat. D phase.

(ii) Neither Mr Herd, the Panel or the LLO had any questions for the witness.

Third Witness (Prison Probation Officer responsible for individual probation work with the prisoner)

(i) Asked by the solicitor if she had anything further to add on the respective merits of release v Cat. D, she supported open prison transfer as a 'period of consolidation'. She was also asked about Mr Herd's response to her work on stress management and on the current role of the home area probation officer.

(ii) The Panel's only initial question concerned whether the witness had discussed the potential 'jump' from Cat. C to a hostel with the home area probation officer.

(iii) The LLO asked the witness to comment further on the factors that could create stress for Mr Herd and to elaborate on the extract of her written report that the prisoner now accepts that he was not ready for open conditions when previously transferred to Cat. D – did this by implication mean that he now felt ready? The Panel then pursued further aspects of the factors considered to be particularly stressful and whether the prisoner was better able to recognise and avoid such triggers.

Closing Statements

(i) Given first opportunity to sum up, the LLO reiterated the case for Cat. D transfer, suggesting that it would be foolhardy to 'go too fast', repeating the previous mistake in transferring Mr Herd prematurely to a stage for which he was not yet ready.

(ii) Prior to summing up for the prisoner, the solicitor was invited to withdraw to take instructions from Mr Herd in private but declined. The solicitor pointed out to the Panel that the prison Parole Clerk who knew Mr Herd well was at the hearing as an observer and was available to be questioned but the Panel declined, indicating that it would not be proper to take the individual by surprise in that way. The solicitor then summarised Mr Herd's prison experience including his previous reasonably successful period in a Cat. D establishment prior to absconding and, in the light of the advantages that immediate release to a hostel could offer in terms of employment, counselling and building community ties, invited the Panel to release him. Failing that, he hoped the Panel might make a firm recommendation for transfer to the open prison favoured by the LLO.

(iii) The Panel had no further questions, indicated to Mr Herd that he would receive its decision within seven days and invited everyone to withdraw.

Comment

It was noticeable how little detailed discussion there was of the prisoner's preferred option of immediate release. The prisoner had decided to make this the basis of his application at quite a late stage. The details were correspondingly somewhat hazy and the plan did not enjoy the wholehearted support of the home area probation officer who was not called as a prisoner's witness. The Panel thus did not have the opportunity to consider the proposal in clear detail, in contrast to which the prisoner's witnesses unanimously supported the Home Secretary's proposal of transfer to open prison. Given this consensus, it was highly unlikely that the Panel would have reached a more cautious view but equally unlikely that the Panel would have the basis for making a more bold decision. It is worth noting that the lifer will not necessarily seek immediate release as the outcome of the DLP Hearing. In another hearing at a Cat. C prison, observed by the author, in which the Home Secretary's view was that the prisoner was not yet ready for lower categorisation, the prisoner sought neither release nor a recommendation of transfer to Cat. D but a recommendation of transfer to an alternative Cat. C establishment nearer his home and a further review after 12 months.

Panel Decision

The Panel considered that Mr Herd needed to learn to display flexibility in respect to the demands and pressures of everyday life and that only a phased rehabilitation programme could offer him this opportunity. The Panel thus decided that he should not be released and instead recommended that he should be transferred to Cat. D conditions, with a specific expectation that he should have the facility of single accommodation and access to the SOTP 'booster' programme. No recommendation was made with regard to the timing of his next review, thus meaning that this would take place in two years' time.

Postscript

On receipt of this decision, Mr Herd reacted badly, thus indicating his continuing problems in handling stress. He subsequently (four months later) received the Secretary of State's decision that he should remain in closed conditions to continue working on his skills in handling stress and that he would be reviewed further under CJA 1991 s32(2) in due course to see whether a move to Cat. D conditions would be appropriate, thus allowing for this possibility prior to his next DLP.

APPENDIX I
PAROLE BOARD RULES 2004

PART 1: INTRODUCTION
Title, commencement and revocation
1. (1) These Rules may be cited as the Parole Board Rules 2004 and shall come into force on 1st August 2004.

   (2) The Parole Board Rules 1997 are hereby revoked.

Application and interpretation
2. (1) Subject to rule 24, these Rules apply where a prisoner's case is referred to the Board by the Secretary of State under section 28(6)(a), 28(7) or 32(4) of the 1997 Act, or under section 39(4) or 44A(2) of the 1991 Act, at any time after the coming into force of these Rules.

   (2) In these Rules, unless a contrary intention appears:

   "Board" means the Parole Board, continued by section 32(1) of the 1991 Act;

   "Chairman" means the chairman of the Board appointed under paragraph 2 of Schedule 5 to the 1991 Act;

   "chair" means the chairman of a panel appointed under rule 3(5);

   "governor" includes a director of a contracted out prison;

   "panel" means those members of the Board constituted in accordance with rule 3 and having conduct of the case;

   "parties" means the prisoner and the Secretary of State;

   "prison" includes a young offender institution or any other institution where the prisoner is or has been detained;

   "single member panel" means that member of the Board constituted in accordance with rule 3(1);

   "three member paper panel" means those members of the Board constituted in accordance with rule 3(2);

   "three member oral panel" means those members of the Board constituted in accordance with rule 3(3);

   "the 1991 Act" means the Criminal Justice Act 1991; and

   "the 1997 Act" means the Crime (Sentences) Act 1997.

PART 2: GENERAL
Appointment of panels

3. (1) The Chairman shall appoint one member of the Board for the purpose of conducting proceedings in relation to a prisoner's case without a hearing pursuant to rule 11.

    (2) Where consideration of a prisoners case is required pursuant to rule 13, the Chairman shall appoint three members of the Board to form a panel for the purpose of conducting proceedings without a hearing pursuant to that rule.

    (3) Subject to paragraph (6) below, where a hearing is required in relation to a prisoner's case, the Chairman shall appoint three members of the Board to form a panel for the purpose of conducting proceedings with a hearing.

    (4) In relation to any prisoners case, no member shall be appointed to more than one of the panels formed under paragraph (1), (2) or (3) above.

    (5) Subject to paragraph (6) below, the Chairman shall appoint one member of each panel to act as chair of that panel.

    (6) In relation to cases referred to the Board under section 28(6)(a), 28(7) or 32(4) of the 1997 Act, the members appointed pursuant to paragraph (3) above shall include a person who has a 5 year general qualification, within the meaning of section 71 of the Courts and Legal Services Act 1990, and that person shall act as chairman of the panel.

Listing the case for hearing

4. The Board shall list the case and shall notify the parties of the date when the case was so listed within 5 working days thereafter.

Representation

5. (1) Subject to paragraph (2), a party may be represented by any person who he has authorised for that purpose.

    (2) The following are ineligible to act as a representative –

    (a) any person liable to be detained under the Mental Health Act 1983,

    (b) any person serving a sentence of imprisonment,

    (c) any person who is on licence having been released under Part III of the Criminal Justice Act 1967, under Part II of the 1991 Act, under Chapter 6 of Part 12 to the Criminal Justice Act 2003 or under Part II of the 1997 Act, or

(d) any person with a previous conviction for an imprisonable offence which remains unspent under the Rehabilitation of Offenders Act 1974.

(3) Within 5 weeks of the case being listed, a party shall notify the Board and the other party of the name, address and occupation of any person authorised in accordance with paragraph (1).

(4) Where a prisoner does not authorise a person to act as his representative, the Board may, with his agreement, appoint someone to act on his behalf.

Information and reports by the Secretary of State

6. (1) Within 8 weeks of the case being listed, the Secretary of State shall serve on the Board and, subject to paragraph (2), the prisoner or his representative –

(a) the information specified in Part A of Schedule 1 to these Rules,

(b) the reports specified in Part B of that Schedule, and

(c) such further information as the Secretary of State considers to be relevant to the case.

(2) Any part of the information or reports referred to in paragraph (1) which, in the opinion of the Secretary of State, should be withheld from the prisoner on the grounds that its dis closure would adversely affect national security, the prevention of disorder or crime or the health or welfare of the prisoner or others (such withholding being a necessary and proportionate measure in all the circumstances of the case), shall be recorded in a separate document and served only on the Board together with the reasons for believing that its disclosure would have that effect.

(3) Where a document is withheld from the prisoner in accordance with paragraph (2), it shall, unless the chair of the panel directs otherwise, nevertheless be served as soon as practicable on the prisoner's representative if he is –

(a) a barrister or solicitor,

(b) a registered medical practitioner, or

(c) a person whom the chair of the panel directs is suitable by virtue of his experience or professional qualification;

provided that no information disclosed in accordance with this paragraph shall be disclosed either directly or indirectly to the prisoner or to any other person without the consent/authority of the chair of the panel.

Evidence of the prisoner

7. (1) Within 12 weeks of the case being listed, the prisoner shall serve on the Board and the Secretary of State any representations about his case that he wishes to make.

    (2) Any other documentary evidence that the prisoner wishes to adduce at a hearing of his case shall be served on the Board and the Secretary of State at least 14 days before the date of the hearing.

Directions

8. (1) Subject to paragraph (4), the chair of the panel may at any time give, vary or revoke such directions as he thinks proper to enable the parties to prepare for the consideration of the prisoners case or to assist the panel to determine the issues.

    (2) Such directions may in particular relate to –

    (a) the timetable for the proceedings,

    (b) the varying of the time within which or by which an act is required by these Rules to be done,

    (c) the service of documents,

    (d) as regards any documents which have been received by the Board but which have been withheld from the prisoner in accordance with rule 6(2), whether withholding such documents is a necessary and proportionate measure in all the circumstances of the case, and

    (e) the submission of evidence.

    (3) Within 7 days of being notified of a direction under paragraph (2)(d), either party may appeal against it to the Chairman, who shall notify the other party of the appeal; the other party may make representations on the appeal to the Chairman whose decision shall be final.

    (4) Directions under paragraph (1) may be given, varied or revoked either –

    (a) of the chair of the panel's own motion, or

    (b) on the written application of a party which has been served on the other party and which specifies the direction that is sought; but in either case, both parties shall be given an opportunity to make written representations or, where the chair of the panel thinks it necessary, and subject to paragraph (7)(b), to make oral submissions at a preliminary hearing fixed in accordance with paragraph (5).

(5) Where the chair of the panel decides to hold a preliminary hearing, he shall give the parties at least 14 days' notice of the date, time and place fixed for that hearing.

(6) A preliminary hearing shall be held in private and information about the proceedings and the names of any persons concerned in the proceedings shall not be made public.

(7) Except in so far as the chair of the panel otherwise directs, at a preliminary hearing –

(a) the chair of the panel shall sit alone, and

(b) the prisoner shall not attend unless he is unrepresented.

(8) The power to give directions may be exercised in the absence of the parties.

(9) Notice of any directions given, varied or revoked under this rule shall be served on the parties as soon as practicable thereafter.

Adjournment

9. (1) The panel may at any time adjourn proceedings to obtain further information or for such other purposes as it may think appropriate

(2) Before adjourning proceedings, the panel may give such directions as it thinks fit to ensure the proceedings can be resumed and the application considered as soon as possible.

(3) Before a three member oral panel resumes any hearing which was adjourned without a further hearing date being fixed, it shall give the parties not less than 3 weeks' notice, or such shorter notice to which all parties may agree, of the date, time and place of the resumed hearing.

Panel decisions

10. (1) Where a panel has been constituted under rule 3(2) or (3), any decision of the majority of the members of the panel shall be the decision of the panel.

(2) For the avoidance of doubt, decisions made pursuant to rule 11(2)(b) or 13(2)(b) are provisional decisions as to the prisoners suitability for release, a final decision only being made pursuant to rule 12(3) or 13(6) or when the case is determined by a three member oral panel.

PART 3: PROCEEDINGS WITHOUT A HEARING
Consideration by single member panel

11. (1) Within 14 weeks of the case being listed, a single member panel shall consider the prisoners case without a hearing.

    (2) The single member panel must either

        (a) decide that the case should be considered by a three member oral panel, or

        (b) make a provisional decision as to the prisoners suitability for release.

    (3) The decision of the single member panel shall be recorded in writing with reasons, and shall be provided to the parties within a week of the date of the decision.

Provisional decision against release

12. (1) In any case where the single member panel has made a provisional decision under rule 11(2)(b) that the prisoner is unsuitable for release, the prisoner may require a three member oral panel to give consideration to his case with a hearing.

    (2) Where the prisoner does so require consideration of his case with a hearing, he must serve notice to that effect on the Board and the Secretary of State within 19 weeks of the case being listed.

    (3) If no notice has been served in accordance with paragraph (2) after the expiry of the period permitted by that paragraph, the provisional decision shall become final and shall be provided to the parties within 20 weeks of the case being listed.

Provisional decision in favour of release: consideration by three member paper panel

13. (1) In any case where the single member panel has made a provisional decision under rule 11(2)(b) that the prisoner is suitable for release, consideration of his case must be made by a three member paper panel within 17 weeks of the case being listed.

    (2) The three member paper panel must either

        (a) decide that the case should be considered by a three member oral panel, or

        (b) uphold the provisional decision of the single member panel that the prisoner is suitable for release.

(3) The decision by the three member paper panel shall be recorded in writing with reasons, and shall be provided to the parties within a week of the date of the decision.

(4) In any case to which paragraph (2)(b) applies, the Secretary of State may require a three member oral panel to give consideration to the prisoners case with a hearing.

(5) Where the Secretary of State does so require consideration of the case with a hearing, he must serve notice to that effect on the Board and the prisoner within 22 weeks of the case being listed.

(6) If no notice has been served in accordance with paragraph (5) after the expiry of the period permitted by that paragraph, the provisional decision shall become final and shall be provided to the parties within 23 weeks of the case being listed.

PART 4: PROCEEDINGS WITH A HEARING
General provisions

14. (1) This Part of the Rules applies in any case where a decision pursuant to rule 11(2)(a) or 13(2)(a) has been made, or where a notice under rule 12(2) or 13(5) has been served, or in any case referred to the Board under section 32(4) of the 1997 Act or under section 39(4) or 44A(2) of the 1991 Act.

(2) In relation to any case to be given consideration by a three member oral panel by virtue of rule 13(5), rule 15(1) shall have effect as if the reference to 20 weeks was a reference to 23 weeks, and rule 15(2) shall have effect as if the reference to 21 weeks was a reference to 24 weeks.

(3) The prisoner shall, within 23 weeks of the case being listed, notify the Board and the Secretary of State whether he wishes to attend the hearing.

(4) Any reference in this Part of the Rules to a panel is to a three member oral panel.

Witnesses

15. (1) Where a party wishes to call witnesses at the hearing, he shall make a written application to the Board, a copy of which he shall serve on the other party, within 20 weeks of the case being listed, giving the name, address and occupation of the witness he wishes to call and the substance of the evidence he proposes to adduce.

(2) Where the Board wishes to call witnesses at the hearing, the chair of the panel should notify the parties, within 21 weeks of the case being listed, giving the name, address and occupation of the witness it wishes to call and the substance of the evidence it proposes to adduce.

(3) The chair of the panel may grant or refuse an application under paragraph (1) and shall communicate his decision to both parties, giving reasons in writing for his decision in the case of a refusal.

(4) Where a witness is called under paragraphs (1) or (2), it shall be the duty of the person calling the witness to notify the witness at least 2 weeks before the hearing of the date of the hearing and the need to attend.

Observers

16. A party may apply, in accordance with the procedure set out in rule 15(1) and (3), to be accompanied at the hearing by such other persons, in addition to any representative he may have authorised, as he wishes to support him or to observe the proceedings; but before granting any such application the Board shall obtain the agreement of –

(a) the governor where the hearing is held in a prison,

(b) in any other case, the person who has the authority to agree.

Notice of hearing

17. (1) The hearing shall be held within 26 weeks of the case being listed, but when fixing the date of the hearing the Board shall consult the parties.

(2) The Board shall give the parties at least 3 weeks notice of the date, time and place scheduled for the hearing or such shorter notice to which the parties may agree.

Location, privacy of proceedings

18. (1) The hearing shall be held at the prison or other institution where the prisoner is detained, or such other place as the chair of the panel, with the agreement of the Secretary of State, may direct.

(2) The hearing shall be held in private.

(3) In addition to witnesses and observers previously approved pursuant to rules 15 and 16, the chair of the panel may admit to the hearing such other persons on such terms and conditions as he considers appropriate.

141

(4) The parties may not challenge at the hearing the attendance of any witness or observer whose attendance has previously been approved pursuant to rules 15 and 16.

Hearing procedure

19. (1) At the beginning of the hearing the chair of the panel shall explain the order of proceeding which the panel proposes to adopt, and shall invite each party present to state their view as to the suitability of the prisoner for release.

(2) The panel shall avoid formality in the proceedings and so far as possible shall make its own enquiries in order to satisfy itself of the level of risk of the prisoner; it shall conduct the hearing in such manner as it considers most suitable to the clarification of the issues before it and generally to the just handling of the proceedings it.

(3) The parties shall be entitled to appear and be heard at the hearing and take such part in the proceedings as the panel thinks fit; and the parties may hear each others evidence, put questions to each other, call any witnesses who the Board has authorised to give evidence in accordance with rule 15, and put questions to any witness or other person appearing before the panel.

(4) The chair of the panel may require any person present at the hearing who is, in his opinion, behaving in a disruptive manner to leave and may permit him to return, if at all, only on such conditions as the chair may specify.

(5) The panel may adduce or receive in evidence any document or information notwithstanding that such document or information would be inadmissible in a court of law, but no person shall be compelled to give any evidence or produce any document which he could not be compelled to give or produce on the trial of an action.

(6) The chair of the panel may require the prisoner, any witness appearing for the prisoner, or any other person present, to leave the hearing where evidence is being examined which the chair of the panel, in accordance with rule 8(2)(d) (subject to any successful appeal under rule 8(2)), previously directed should be withheld from the prisoner as adversely affecting national security, the prevention of disorder or crime or the health or welfare of the prisoner or others.

(7) After all the evidence has been given, the prisoner shall be given a further opportunity to address the panel.

The decision

20. The panels decision determining a case shall be recorded in writing with reasons, signed by the chair of the panel, and provided in writing to the parties not more than 7 days after the end of the hearing; the recorded decision with reasons shall only make reference to matters which the Secretary of State has referred to the Board.

PART 5: MISCELLANEOUS

Time

21. Where the time prescribed by or under these Rules for doing any act expires on a Saturday, Sunday or public holiday, the act shall be in time if done on the next working day.

Transmission of documents etc.

22. Any document required or authorised by these Rules to be served or otherwise transmitted to any person may be transmitted by electronic means, sent by pre-paid post or delivered –

(a) in the case of a document directed to the Board or the chair of the panel, to the office of the Board;

(b) in any other case, to the last known address of the person to whom the document is directed.

Irregularities

23. Any irregularity resulting from a failure to comply with these Rules before the panel has determined a case shall not of itself render the proceedings void, but the panel may, and shall, if it considers that the person may have been prejudiced, take such steps as it thinks fit, before determining the case, to cure the irregularity, whether by the amendment of any document, the giving of any notice, the taking of any step or otherwise.

References to the Board following recall

24. (1) Where the Secretary of State refers a prisoner's case to the Board under section 32(4) of the 1997 Act or section 39(4) of the 1991 Act to consider a recall:

(a) rules 11 to 13 shall not apply; and

(b) subject to the above, these Rules shall only apply where the prisoner has made representations against recall and subject to the modifications in paragraph (2).

(2) The modifications referred to in paragraph (1) are as follows:

(a) any references to periods of time set out in these Rules shall apply as if they were references to such period of time as the chair of the panel shall in each case determine, taking into account both the desirability of the Board reaching an early decision in the prisoner's case and the need to ensure fairness to the prisoner; and

(b) rule 6 shall apply as if the references in paragraph (1)(a) and (b) of that rule to the information and reports specified in Schedule 1 were references to the information and reports set out in Schedule 2.

Transitional provision

25. The revocation by these Rules of the Parole Board Rules 1997 does not affect their operation in relation to any referral of a prisoners case made to the Board before the coming into force of the revocation.

Home Office 2004 Parliamentary Under-Secretary of State

SCHEDULE 1: INFORMATION AND REPORTS FOR SUBMISSION TO THE BOARD BY THE SECRETARY OF STATE ON A REFERENCE TO THE BOARD UNDER SECTION 28(6)(A) OR (7) OF THE 1997 ACT OR SECTION 44A(2) OF THE 1991 ACT [RULE 6(1)]

PART A: INFORMATION RELATING TO THE PRISONER

1. The full name of the prisoner

2. The date of birth of the prisoner.

3. The prison in which the prisoner is detained and details of other prisons in which the prisoner has been detained, the date and reasons for any transfer.

4. The date the prisoner was given the life sentence or extended sentence, details of the offence and any previous convictions.

5. The comments, if available, of the trial judge in passing sentence.

6. Where applicable, the conclusions of the Court of Appeal in respect of any appeal by the prisoner against conviction or sentence.

7. The parole history, if any, of the prisoner, including details of any periods spent on licence during the currency of the life sentence or extended sentence.

PART B: REPORTS RELATING TO THE PRISONER

1. Pre-trial and pre-sentence reports examined by the sentencing court on the circumstances of the offence.

2. Reports on a prisoner while he was subject to a transfer direction under section 47 of the Mental Health Act 1983.

3. Current reports on the prisoners risk factors, reduction in risk and performance and behaviour in prison, including views on suitability for release on licence as well as compliance with any sentence plan.

4. An up-to-date home circumstances report prepared for the Board by an officer of the supervising local probation board, including information on the following where relevant:

(a) details of the home address, family circumstances, and family attitudes towards the prisoner;

(b) alternative options if the offender cannot return home;

(c) the opportunity for employment on release;

(d) the local communitys attitude towards the prisoner (if known);

(e) the attitudes and concerns of the victims of the offence (if known);

(f) the prisoners attitude to the index offence;

(g) the prisoners response to previous periods of supervision;

(h) the prisoners behaviour during any temporary leave during the current sentence;

(i) the prisoners attitude to the prospect of release and the requirements and objectives of supervision;

(j) an assessment of the risk of reoffending;

(k) a programme of supervision;

(l) a view on suitability for release; and

(m) recommendations regarding any non-standard licence conditions.

SCHEDULE 2: INFORMATION AND REPORTS FOR SUBMISSION TO THE BOARD BY THE SECRETARY OF STATE ON A REFERENCE TO THE BOARD UNDER SECTION 32(4) OF THE 1997 ACT OR SECTION 39(4) OF THE 1991 ACT [RULES 6(1) AND 24(2)(B)]

PART A: INFORMATION RELATING TO THE PRISONER

1. The full name of the prisoner.

2. The date of birth of the prisoner.

3. The prison in which the prisoner is detained and details of other prisons in which the prisoner has been detained, the date and reasons for any transfer.

4. The date the prisoner was given the life sentence or extended sentence, details of the offence and any previous convictions.

5. The parole history, if any, of the prisoner, including details of any periods spent during the currency of the life sentence or extended sentence.

6. In the case of a referral under section 32(4) of the 1997 Act, the details of any life sentence plan prepared for the prisoner which have previously been disclosed to him.

7. The details of any previous recalls of the prisoner including the reasons for such recalls and subsequent re-release on licence.

8. The statement of reasons for the most recent recall which was given to the prisoner under section 32(3)(b) of the 1997 Act or section 39(3)(b) of the 1991 Act.

9. The details of any memorandum which the Board considered prior to making its recommendation for recall under section 32(1) of the 1997 Act or section 39(1) of the 1991 Act, or confirming the Secretary of States decision to recall under section 32(2) of the 1997 Act or section 39(2) of the 1991 Act, including the reasons why the Secretary of State considered it expedient in the public interest to recall that person before it was practicable to obtain a recommendation from the Board.

PART B: REPORTS RELATING TO THE PRISONER

1. The reports considered by the Board prior to making its recommendation for recall under section 32(1) of the 1997 Act or section 39(1) of the 1991 Act, or its confirmation of the Secretary of States decision to recall under section 32(2) of the 1997 Act or section 39(2) of the 1991 Act.

2. Any reports considered by the Secretary of State in deciding to recall under section 32(2) of the 1997 Act or section 39(2) of the 1991 Act.

3. In the case of a referral under section 39(4) of the 1991 Act, any pre-sentence report examined by the sentencing court on the circumstances of the offence.

4. Any other relevant reports.

APPENDIX II
ADVICE SERVICES FOR LIFERS

'Justice'

59 Carter Lane, London EC4V 5AQ, 020 7329 5100

JUSTICE, the British section of the International Commission of Jurists, is an independent organisation which campaigns for reforms in the criminal justice system to ensure fairness and prevent miscarriages. It receives over 600 enquiries a year from people claiming to be victims of miscarriages of justice and undertakes detailed investigations into over 100 cases a year, assisting with the presentation of appeals and (pending the introduction of the CCRC) petitions to the Home Office, in cases where the individual is serving a long prison sentence and is not legally aided.

The Prisoners' Advice Service

PO Box 46199, London EC1M 4XA, 020 7253 3323/0845 430 8923

Launched in 1991, the Prisoners' Advice Service charity provides advice and information to prisoners in England and Wales regarding their rights, particularly concerning the application of the *Prison Rules* and the conditions of their imprisonment, taking up prisoners' complaints about their treatment within the prison system and supporting applications for transfers, temporary release, parole and compassionate release. Lifers constituted 7% of enquiries dealt with in the year September 1993 to August 1994. PAS act for many mandatory lifers both at the time their tariffs are set and at the time of their reviews, making representations to the Parole Board and the Home Secretary. PAS is not able to represent discretionary lifers facing DLP hearings but has issued applications to the European Commission of Human Rights.

Justice for Women

c/o 55 Rathcoole Gardens, London N8 9NE, 07930 824414

Justice for Women is a feminist organisation which campaigns against discrimination within the legal system towards women subjugated to male violence. Among its aims it 'publicises and challenges the outcome of specific cases where women or children who have suffered male violence have been unfairly treated'. It will thus assist women convicted of murder of a violent man in circumstances where the killing can be regarded as an act of 'self-preservation'.

APPENDIX III
IPP AND LIFE SENTENCE FORMS

Form	Completed by	Timescale
POSTSRA Brief report with further information not contained in PSR	OM	In time for Initial Sentence Planning and Risk Management Meeting
POSTSRB When no PSR is prepared	OM	In time for Initial Sentence Planning and Risk Management Meeting.
OM A Probation to Prison informing prison of name and contact details of OM	OM	Within 5 working days of sentence
OM B Prison to Probation with contact details of OS	OS	Within 5 working days of reception
OM C OS gives to prisoner informing him/her of details of OS and OM	OS	In a timely manner
OM D Protecting Positive Factors interview with prisoner	OS	In a timely manner
OM E Exchange of information not covered by other forms	OS OR OM	When required
OM F Notifying OM of prisoner transfer	OS	Within 5 working days of transfer
OM G Notifies OM of name and contact details of new allocated OS	OS in receiving prison	Within 5 working days of receipt of prisoner
LISP 1 Initial notification and post sentence interview of prisoner	OS	Within 7 working days of sentence
LISP 2 Record of MARAP meeting	OS	On completion of meeting
LISP 3 Record of escorted absence and ROTL	OS	In a timely manner
LISP 4 Failure report in open conditions, ROTL	OS	In a timely manner

LISP 5 Escorted absence report Escorting officer sends report to OS and copies OM	Officer escorting prisoner	In a timely manner
LISP 6 Recall notification and induction interview which is then forwarded to Post Release Section	OM	Within 7 days of recall
SP 1 Requesting OS arrange sentence planning meeting	OM	In a timely manner.
SP2 Invitation to internal prison and external agencies/partnerships to attend sentence planning	OS	In a timely manner
SPR A Sentence planning progress documentation cover	OS	In time for Sentence Planning meeting
SPR B Progress Report (PAROM 1 for Parole Review)	OM	In time for Sentence Planning meeting or parole review
SPR C Progress report	OS	In time for Sentence Planning meeting
SPR D Progress report	Key Worker	In time for Sentence Planning meeting
SPR E Progress report	Psychologist	In time for Sentence Planning meeting
SPR F Progress report Information disclosed must be within the limits of patient confidentiality and countersigned by Senior Medical Officer	Healthcare	In time for Sentence Planning meeting
SPR G Progress report	Psychiatrist	In time for Sentence Planning meeting
SPR J Progress report (offender comments)	Offender	In time for Sentence Planning meeting
SPR K Progress report	Lifer Manager	In time for Sentence Planning meeting
SPR H Security Report. Information is disclosed to offender unless there is a non-disclosure application (PSO 6000 or Parole Board Rule 6)	Prison Security Officer	In time for Sentence Planning meeting.

SENTENCES FOR DANGEROUS OFFENDERS

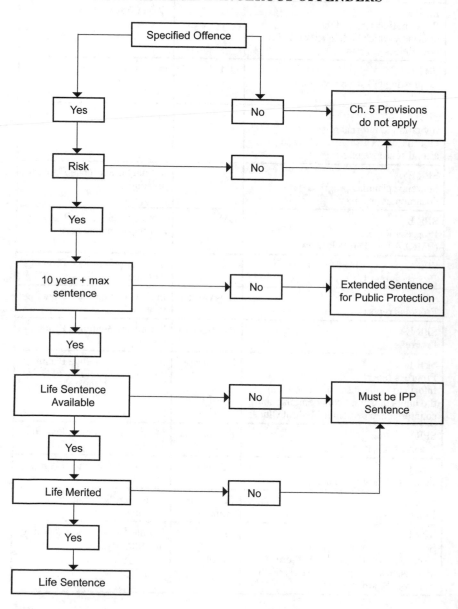

REFERENCES

Aubrey, C. and A. Hossack (1994). 'Contacting Victims of Life Sentence Crimes', *Probation Journal* 41(4): 212–14.

Aust, A. (1996). 'A Practitioner View of Risk: A Case Study for Life Licence'. *Good Practice in Risk Assessment and Risk Management.* Eds. H. Kemshall and J. Pritchard. London: Jessica Kingsley Publishers.

Baird, V. (1996). 'Mandatory Thought Required'. *Criminal Justice* 14(2): 4–5.

Barak-Glanty, I.L. (1981). 'Toward a Conceptual Scheme of Prison Management Styles'. *The Prison Journal* 61(2).

Barter, S. (1995). 'Discretionary Lifers: Tariffs and Discretionary Lifer Panels'. *Probation Journal* 42(3): 140–45.

Barter, S. (1996). 'Pre-Release Work with Life Sentence Prisoners: Lessons from a Pre-Release Employment Hostel'. *Probation Journal* 43(4).

Blunkett, D. (2006). *The Blunkett Tapes: My Life in the Bearpit.* London: Bloomsbury.

Bolton, N. *et al* (1976). 'Psychological Correlates of Long-Term Imprisonment'. *BJ Criminology* 16.

Boswell, G. (1996). *Young and Dangerous.* Avebury.

Brown, L. *et al.* (1990). *Families of Murder Victims Project: Final Report.* Victim Support.

Burgess, A. (1975). 'Family Reaction to Homicide'. *American Journal of Orthopsychiatry* 45(3), 39–98.

Burgess, A. and L. Holmstrom (1974). 'Rape Trauma Syndrome'. *American Journal of Psychiatry* 131(9): 981–96.

Casey, M. (1996). 'Lifers and the SOTP', *Prison Report* 34, 24.

Celnick, A., and W. McWilliams (1991). 'Helping, Treating and Doing Good'. *Probation Journal* 4(38).

Clark D. *et al* (1993). 'A New Methodology for Assessing the Level of Risk in Incarcerated Offenders', *B.J. Criminology* 33: 436–48.

Cohen S. and L. Taylor (1981). *Psychological Survival: The Experience of Long-Term Imprisonment.* Penguin.

Coker, J. and J. Martin (1985). *Licensed to Live.* Basil Blackwell.

Council of Europe (Committee on Crime Problems) (1977). *Treatment of Long-Term Prisoners*.

Coyle, A. (2005). 'On being a Prisoner in the United Kingdom in the 21st Century'. *Prison Service Journal* 162.

Crawley, E. (2005). 'Surviving the prison experience? Imprisonment & Elderly Men'. *Prison Service Journal* 160.

Creighton, S. (1996). 'Sentences of HMP', *Legal Action*, June: 20–21.

Creighton, S. and V. King (1995). 'The Law Relating to Prisoners: Mandatory Lifers'. *Legal Action*: 13–15.

Creighton, S. and V. King (1996). *Prisoners and the Law*. Butterworths.

Donaldson, (Lord) (1996). 'An Unwise Path'. *The Guardian*, 4 April 1996.

Dooley, E. (1990). 'Prison Suicide in England and Wales 1972–87'. *BJ Psychiatry* 156: 40–45.

Flanagan, T. (1980). 'The Pains of Long-Term Imprisonment'. *BJ Criminology* 20: 148–56.

Flanagan, T. (1981). 'Dealing with Long-Term Confinement: Adaptive Strategies and Perspective among Long-Term Prisoners'. *Criminal Justice and Behaviour* 8(3): 201–22.

Friendship, C., R. Mann and A. Beech (2003). *The Prison-Based Sex Offender Treatment Programme – An Evaluation*. Home Office Report 205. London.

Genders, E. and E. Player (1988). 'Women Lifers: Assessing the Experience'. *Women and the Penal System*. Eds A. Morris and C. Wilkinson. Cropwood Conference Series No.19, Institute of Criminology, Cambridge.

Gibson, B. (2004). *Criminal Justice Act 2003: A Guide to the New Procedures and Sentencing*. Winchester: Waterside Press.

Grey, S. (1996). 'A Lacuna Closed for Discretionary Life Sentence Prisoners'. *New Law Journal*: 568–69.

Gunn, J. *et al* (1991). *Mentally Disordered Prisoners*. Home Office.

Harris, V. (1991). 'The Lifer System: Future Developments. *Proceedings of Psychology Conference*. October 1991, Home Office.

HM Chief Inspector of Prisons (1996a). *HMP Durham: Report of a Full Inspection*. Home Office.

HM Chief Inspector of Prisons (1996b). *HMP Gartree: Report of a Full Inspection*, Home Office.

HM Inspectorate of Probation (1995). *Dealing with Dangerous People: The Probation Service and Public Protection.* Home Office.

HM Inspectorate of Probation (1996a). *Report of Home Office Seminar* (6 December 1995) on HMIP Thematic Report 'Dealing with Dangerous People', Home Office.

HM Inspectorate of Probation (1996b). *Suffolk Probation Service: Quality and Effectiveness Inspection Report No. 18.* Home Office.

Home Office (2006). *Guidance on the Implementation of Practice Recommendations from HMIP Independent Review of Serious Further Offences.* Probation Circular 15/2006.

Home Office (2006(a)). *Making Sentences Clearer. A Consultation and Report of a Review by the Home Secretary, Lord Chancellor and Attorney General.* Home Office. London.

Home Office (2006(b)). *Partial Implementation of Sections 14 and 15 (1) & (2) of CJA 2003.* Home Office Circular 039/2006. Home Office. London.

Home Offfice (2006(c)). *Rebalancing the criminal justice system in favour of the law abiding majority.* Cutting crime, reducing re-offending and protecting the public. Home Office. London.

Home Office (2005). *The Resettlement of Discretionary Life-Sentenced Offenders.* Home Office Development & Practice Report 44. London.

Home Office (1996). *Protecting the Public: The Government's Strategy on Crime in England and Wales,* Cm 3190, HMSO.

Home Office (1994). 'Life Licensees and Restricted Patients Reconvictions: England Wales 1991', *Home Office Statistical Bulletin* 18/94, Government Statistical Service (1994).

Hood, R. and S. Shute (1996). 'Protecting the Public: Automatic Life Sentences, Parole and High Risk Offenders'. *Crim LR:* 788–800.

Hood, R. & S. Shute (2000). *The Parole System at Work: a Study of Risk-based Decision Making.* Home Office Research Study 2002. London.

Hornby, S. (2007). *Loving Men? An Exploratory Study of Men's Sexual Experience in UK Prisons.* Unpublished Thesis. University of Cambridge.

House of Commons Select Committee on Home Affairs (1995). *Murder: The Mandatory Life Sentence.* HMSO.

House of Commons Select Committee on Home Affairs (1996). *Murder: The Mandatory Life Sentence (2nd Report).* HMSO.

House of Lords (1989). *Report of the Select Committee on Murder and Life Imprisonment* (Chairman: Lord Nathan) HL Paper 78 I-III, Session 1988–89, HMSO.

Howard League for Penal Reform (2007). 'Indeterminate Sentences for Public Protection'. *Prison Bulletin* 3. www.howardleague.org

Hulme, C. (2000). *Manslaughter United*. London: Yellow Jersey Press.

Jewkes, Y. (2002). *Captive Audience. Media, Masculinity & Power in Prisons*. Cullompton: Willan.

Jewkes, Y. (2005). 'Loss, Liminality and the Life Sentence: managing identity through a disrupted life course'. *The Effects of Imprisonment*. Eds. A. Liebling and S. Maruna. Cullompton: Willan.

Johnston, P. (1994). *The Victim's Charter and the Release of Life Sentence Prisoners: Implications for Probation Service Practice, Values and Management*. Institute of Criminology, University of Cambridge.

Johnston, P. (1995). 'The Victim's Charter and the Release of Long Term Prisoners'. *Probation Journal* 42(1): 8–12.

Justice (1996a). 'Children and Homicide: Appropriate Procedures for Juveniles in Murder and Manslaughter Cases'. *Justice*.

Justice (1996b). 'Sentenced for Life: Reform of the Law and Procedure for those Sentenced to Life Imprisonment'. *Justice*.

Kershaw, C., Dowdeswell, P. and J. Goodman (1997). 'Life Licensees – Reconvictions & Recalls by the End of 1995: England and Wales'. *Home Office Study* 2/97. London.

Kilpatrick, D. *et al* (1989). 'Victim and Crime Factors Associated with the Development of Crime-Related Post-Traumatic Stress Disorder'. *Behaviour Therapy* 20: 199–214.

King R. and K. Elliott (1977). *Albany: Birth of a Prison*. Routledge.

Knight, C. (1996). 'Who Supports the Workers?'. *Probation Journal* 43(3): 132–36.

Lane (Lord) (Chair) (1993). *Report of Committee on the Penalty for Homicide*. Prison Reform Trust.

Law K. (1993). *A Retrospective Study of the Efficiency of the HMP Wakefield Risk Assessment Proforma with Life Licensees*, unpublished MSc dissertation.

Lawton, J. (1978). 'Some Lifers' Views'. *Prison Service Journal*. April 1978: 9–10.

Livingstone, S. and T. Owen (1993). *Prison Law: Text and Materials*. Clarendon Press.

McDougall, C. and D. Clark (1991). 'A Risk Assessment Model'. *Proceedings of Psychology Conference*. October 1991, Home Office.

McFarlane, M. (1995). 'Contact between Long Term Prisoners and Prison Probation Officers'. *Probation Journal* 42(2): 73–8.

McGeorge, N.(1990). *A Fair Deal for LU*. Quaker Council for European Affairs.

MacKenzie, D. *et al* (1989). 'Long-Term Incarceration of Female Offenders: Prison Adjustment and Coping'. *Criminal Justice and Behaviour* 16(2): 223–38.

Malleson, K. (1995). The Criminal Cases Review Commission: How 'Will It Work?' *Crim LR*: 929–37.

Marshall, L. (1996). 'Muzzling the Watchdog'. *Prison Report*: 35, 28.

Mitchell, B. (1990). *Murder and Penal Policy*. Macmillan.

Mitchell, B. (1992). 'Preparing Life Sentence Prisoners for Release', *Howard Journal* 31(3): 224–39.

Morrissey, C. (1995). 'Groupwork with Life Sentence Prisoners'. *Groupwork in Prisons* (Issues in Criminological and Legal Psychology No. 23). Ed. G. Towl. British Psychological Society.

National Probation Service (2005). *CJA 2003 National Implementation Guide for Probation*, Edition 2.

Newburn, T. (1993). 'The Long-Term Needs of Victims. A Review of the Literature'. *Research and Planning Unit Paper 80*. Home Office.

Newton, I. (1995). 'Whole Life Tariff and Review: The New Arrangements'. *Lifer News*, Spring 1995.

Padfield, N. (1995). 'Life Sentences Revisited'. *Archbold News 8*. 4 October 1995: 57.

Padfield, N. (1996(a)). 'The Mandatory Life Sentence in the Balance', *New Law Journal*. 26 January 1996: 98–99.

Padfield, N. (1996(b)). 'Bailing and Sentencing the Dangerous'. *Dangerous People*. Ed. N. Walker, Blackstone Press.

Page, J. (1995). 'Presenting Cases to Discretionary Lifer Panels'. *Lifer News* 2, Summer 1995, HM Prison Service.

Parker, T. (1990). *Life After Life*. Secker and Warburg.

Parker, T. (1995). *The Violence of Our Lives*. Harper Collins.

Probation Circular 27 (2007). Victim Representation at Parole Board Hearings.

Probation Circular 29 (2007). Post Release Enforcement – Licence Conditions.

PSO 6300 (2005). Release on Temporary Licence. London.

Penal Affairs Consortium (1995). *Sentencing and Early Release: The Home Secretary's Proposals*. PAC.

Penal Affairs Consortium (1996). *The 'Supermax' Option*. PAC.

Porporino, F. and Zamble, E. (1984). 'Coping with Imprisonment'. *Canadian Journal of Criminology* 26(4): 403–21.

Prins, H. (1995). 'Risk Assessment: Seven Sins of Omission'. *Probation Journal* 42(4): 199–201.

Prison Governors Association (1995). *A Manifesto for Change*. PGA.

Prison Reform Trust (1995). *A Suitable Case for Treatment? The Penile Plethysmograph and the Assessment of Potential Sex Offenders*. PRT.

Raban, T. *et al* (1983). *Work with Life Sentence Prisoners at Nottingham Prison*. Nottinghamshire Probation Service.

Richards, E. (1978). 'The Experience of Long-Term Imprisonment'. *BJ Criminology* 18: 162–8.

Rijnenberg, B. (2007). Will the Reducing Re-offending Action Plan Make Prisoners' Children the 'Visible' Victims of Crime? Unpublished thesis. University of Cambridge.

Rose, D. (1995). 'Lawyers Alarmed at Lenient Sentences for Serial Rapists'. *The Observer*, 26 November 1995.

Sapsford, R. (1978). 'Life Sentence Prisoners: Psychological Changes During Sentence'. *BJ Criminology* 18, 128–45.

Sapsford, R. (1983). *Life Sentence Prisoners*. Open University Press.

Sapsford, R. and C. Banks (1979). 'A Synopsis of Some Home Office Research' in Smith D. (ed) *Life Sentence Prisoners*, Home Office Research Unit Study No.51, HMSO.

Sentencing Guidelines Council (2007). Reduction in Sentence for a Guilty Plea. Definitive Guideline. SGC. London.

Shannon, T. and C. Morgan (1996). *Invisible Crying Tree*. Doubleday.

Shute, S. (2006). 'Punishing Murderers. Release Procedures and the 'Tariff' – 1953/2004'. *Prison Service Journal* 164, March 2006.

Slatter, G. (2006). Home Office Research Study No. 231: 'Rates and Causes of Death among Prisoners and Offenders under Community Supervision'. Home Office. London, 2006.

Stone N. (1995). *A Companion Guide to Mentally Disordered Offenders*. Owen Wells Publisher.

Stone, N. (2006). 'Dangerous Offenders'. *Probation Journal* 53(2).

Straw, J. (1996). *Honesty, Consistency and Progression in Sentencing*. Labour Party.

Swinton, M. *et al* (1994). 'Psychiatric Disorder and Life-Sentence Prisoners'. *Criminal Behaviour and Mental Health* 4(1): 10–20.

Taylor, P. (1986). 'Psychiatric Disorder in London's Life-Sentence Prisoners'. *BJ Criminology* 26: 63–78.

Taylor, R. (2003). 'An Assessment of Violent Incident Rates on the Dangerous and Severe Personality Disorder Unit at HMP Whitemoor'. *Home Office Study* 210. London.

Taylor, R., M. Wasik, and R. Leng (2004). *Blackstone's Guide to the CJA 2003*. Oxford: OUP.

Thomas, D. (1992). 'The Criminal Justice Act 1991: Custodial Sentences'. *Crim LR*: 232–39.

Thomas, D. (1995). 'Blind Man's Buff'. *The Guardian*. 4 December 1995.

Truscott, J. (1995). 'Life Sentence Prisoners and Suicide'. *Life Support*.

United Nations (1994). 'Life Imprisonment'. Crime Prevention and Criminal Justice Branch, Vienna, ST/CSDHA/24.

Vanstone, M. (2004). 'Mission Control. The Origins of a Humanitarian Service'. *Probation Journal* 5/1.

Whittington, J. (1994). 'Lifers, Long Term Prisoners and Education'. *Prison Service Journal*, November: 45–51.

Williams, B. (1991). 'Probation Contact with Long Term Prisoners'. *Probation Journal* 38(1): 4–9.

Windlesham (Lord) (1989). 'Life Sentences: The Paradox of Indeterminacy'. *Crim LR*: 244–56.

Windlesham (Lord) (1993). 'Life Sentences: Law, Practice and Release Decisions 1989–93'. *Crim LR*: 644–59.

Windlesham (Lord) (1993). *Responses to Crime: Penal Policy in the Making.* Volume 2. Oxford University Press.

Windlesham (Lord) (1996). 'Life Sentences: The Case for Assimilation'. *Crim LR*: 250–54.

Zamble, E. (1992). 'Behaviour and Adaptation in Long Term Prison Inmates', *Criminal Justice and Behaviour* 19(4): 409–25.

'Zeno' (1968). *Life.* Macmillan.